UPS Handbook

UPS Handbook

A Layman's Guide to Uninterruptible Power Supply Systems

ROBERT DE LAUTER, PE

QUIRAUK MOUNTAIN PUBLISHING
FREDERICK

UPS Handbook Copyright © 2020 by Robert De Lauter, PE. All Rights Reserved.

Dedication

To my sons, Matthew and Cooper. Because of you, I am a better person.

Contents

Before We Begin ix

Part I. The UPS System

1. Introduction 3
2. UPS 101-The Basics 7
3. Operating Modes 15
4. More UPS Components 19
5. UPS System Voltage Options 29
6. Control Logic Circuits 34
7. UPS Topologies 37
8. Power Problems 45
9. Misunderstood Concepts 54
10. UPS Configurations: Single and Parallel 60
11. Modular UPS systems 69
12. How to Achieve Availability 76
13. Maintenance 81
14. When to Hire a Consultant 84

Part II. Batteries

15. Introduction 91
16. Types of Lead-Acid Batteries 94
17. Choosing the Right Battery System 96
18. Battery Maintenance 100
19. Long Run Times: A Case Study 104
20. Summary of Other Technologies 106

Conclusion	109
Acknowledgments	110
About the Author	112

Before We Begin

How to Use This Book

As with any book, a person could read it from cover to cover. However, I imagine it being used as more of a resource. Please take a few moments to review the table of contents and read the sections you need to understand at the moment.

I hope that you not only pick up useful information but are also slightly entertained by the material provided. Although few people typically find engineering books entertaining, I've tried to make the material interesting and perhaps even humorous from time to time.

This book does not go into deep detail on many subjects, but instead covers the basics and allows the reader to speak the same language as others in the industry.

Feel free to contact me with any questions or feedback.

rob@robdelauter.com

Safety

Reading this book does not provide the qualifications to work on or near electrical equipment, including UPS systems. UPS systems are complicated and power is supplied from multiple sources. It's critical that only people trained in the electrical industry service this equipment. Unqualified persons performing electrical work can result in severe injury, including death.

Operation can be completed by individuals not electrically qualified; however, they must be trained in how to work the specific system. Each system functions differently and mis-operation can damage the system and lead to a loss of power to the critical load.

PART I
THE UPS SYSTEM

1. Introduction

What is an uninterruptible power supply—or UPS system—and why do we need one? If you are reading this book, you probably have a basic understanding of its purpose and necessity.

Critical equipment, such as phone systems, IT equipment, and fiber optics require continuous power to operate. If they lose electrical power for even a fraction of a second, they will shut down. Often it takes minutes or even hours to restart them. Sometimes there is damage to the equipment that requires repairs before the system will work again.

Facebook, Amazon, banks, and credit card companies use UPS systems to keep their operations running twenty-four hours a day, seven days a week, 365 days a year.

Television and radio stations also use UPS systems to be sure they can transmit continuously.

There is a good chance that your company has a UPS system of some size to keep your email and interoffice servers working in the event of a power problem.

What is a Static UPS System?

The Institute of Electrical and Electronics Engineers (IEEE) defines a Static UPS system as "an electronically controlled solid-state system designed to provide an alternate source of conditioned, reliable, and break-free electrical power to a user's equipment." So, what does this mean to non-engineers?

As its name implies, it is a system that provides uninterrupted power. It is an electrical device that supplies constant power to critical load equipment. Put another way, a UPS system is a device that, when the utility power fails, ensures that your computers keep humming along. But it is not always computers; it can be any electrical equipment that can't afford to lose power.

When I interview someone for a field service position, one of my first questions is, "Have you reviewed what we do here?" Nine out of ten times the answer is yes, you do something with battery backup. From this I explain what a UPS system is.

I use a simple black box with two inputs and one output. The inputs are normal alternating current (AC) power and emergency direct current (DC) power, while the output is AC power that supports critical electrical equipment during a power outage. The UPS system is provided input power from an external source, normally the utility company. (See Figure 1.)

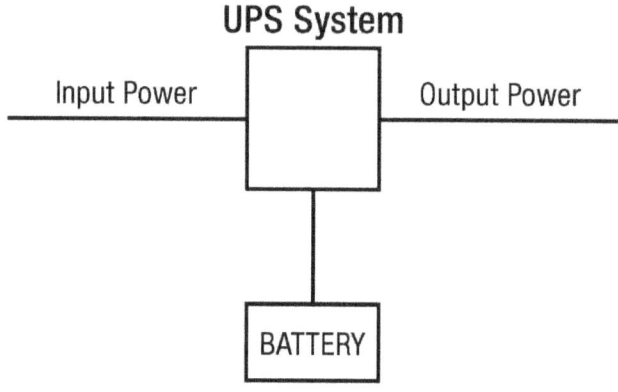

Figure 1

If the UPS system senses a loss of input power, it will automatically switch to battery power and keep the critical load operating. How this switch occurs depends on the type of

UPS topology, which we discuss more in the chapter **UPS System Topologies**.

UPS System or Generator?

A common question asked is, "I have generator; why do I need a UPS system?" Or the reverse, "If I have a UPS system, why do I need a generator?"

A UPS system and a generator are different tools, and each should be used for its specific purpose. Like all tools, you can use the wrong one and do the job, but not as effectively as if you made the correct choice. UPS systems are used for short outages or as a bridge to get from utility power to generator power. (See Figure 2.)

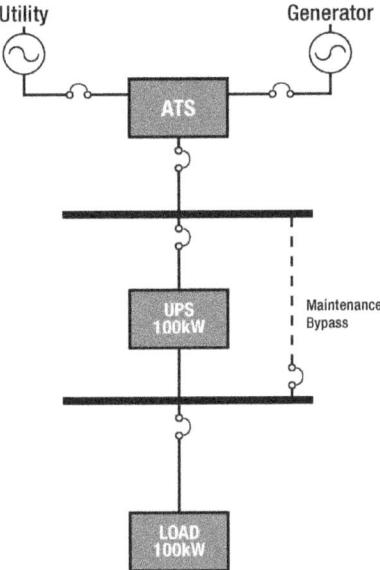

Figure 2

UPS systems primarily use batteries to operate during the outage. Batteries only last so long before they run out of power. As we will discuss later, batteries have a finite life, are expensive, and require maintenance.

UPS systems have a limited run time while on batteries. They are designed and installed with a specific battery backup time. Often you will hear fifteen minutes, but the length of time depends on how much power is required to perform whatever task is needed if power is not restored in the required time.

For all intents and purposes, a generator will run as long as it has a fuel source and doesn't break down. A UPS system can only operate without input power for as long as the batteries last. This translates to: a generator can support the loads as long as necessary, whereas the UPS can only support as long as it has battery power.

Generators are mechanical devices with engines that take several seconds to start and produce electrical power. The best ones can accomplish this within ten seconds, but in electrical time ten seconds is an eternity, and critical equipment cannot be without electrical power that long.

If an outage lasts more than a few seconds, the generator will start and begin to supply power to the UPS system. Often there are other systems—such as lights and air conditioning—on the generator. It is not considered good practice for many of these systems to be powered by a UPS system. Air conditioners and other motor loads draw high current when starting, known as inrush. This high inrush current can cause the UPS system to overload and transfer to bypass leaving the load unprotected to power outages.

2. UPS 101-The Basics

Double Outage: A Case Study

Several years ago, a colleague and I were completing preventive maintenance on an older UPS system. While transferring the system to External Maintenance Bypass, the system failed, causing a back-feed that tripped an upstream feed circuit breaker. When this circuit breaker tripped, the power to the Automatic Transfer Switch (ATS) and the load was lost. This loss in power to the ATS started the generator.

It first became apparent to us that the customer misunderstood the system when the facility personnel reset the input circuit breaker, restoring power to the critical load. The UPS system was still in bypass while discussions took place with site operations. Once the circuit breaker was re-closed, the ATS started its thirty-minute clock, checking that input power was good. At the end of the thirty minutes, the ATS would transfer the load back to utility power and the generator would shut down.

My colleague and I tried to explain to the management team that they needed to keep the circuit breaker open until the UPS system could be repaired, but we were not making ourselves clear, and the clock continued to tick.

After thirty minutes, the customer had restarted nearly eighty percent of the equipment. The ATS transferred the load back utility. This resulted in a total loss of power to all critical loads for about two seconds, more than four hundred times longer than the equipment could handle.

It can be seen in Figure 3 that the UPS system was not available to bridge the gap during the transfer from the generator back to the utility. The customer was furious and could not understand why, if they had a generator, they would lose power again.

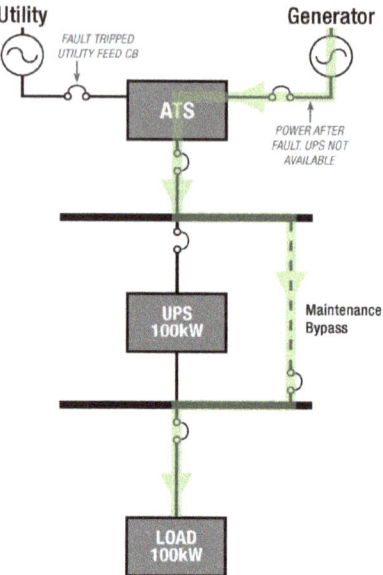

Figure 3

Once the systems were restored and the UPS system repaired, many meetings between our team and theirs ensued. This customer is now well versed in the various operating conditions of not only the UPS system but also the entire critical power system. If they had understood even the basics of how the generator and UPS system interacted, they would have only experienced one outage that day.

I hope that after reading this book, you will have a better understanding of how your UPS system works and how it fits into your overall electrical infrastructure, most importantly, how each of the operational statuses—including failures—affects the critical load.

The most important thing to understand about a UPS system is its operating condition and what that means to the critical load. When talking about a UPS system's operating condition, everyone must be on the same page. Countless times customers ask if we are shutting off their system. Often a new technician will say "yes." The technician is correct; depending on the type of maintenance, the UPS unit will be shut down. But what the customer is asking is will their load be turned off. This question is more difficult to answer.

When we understand what condition the UPS system will be in, we can understand the risks involved to our critical load.

If you get nothing else from this book, this is the section that is most important to understand, and it starts with everyone speaking the same language.

Major Components

As was just explained in the previous section, one of the most important things to understand about your UPS system is what mode of operation it is in. Before we dive into understanding the different modes of operation, we should take a few minutes to review the major building blocks or components of a UPS system.

An in-depth explanation of how rectifiers, inverters, and other power electronics work is not needed for most people when understanding their UPS system, but we must possess a basic understanding of what the major building blocks do and how they interact with each other.

The most complicated system is the double conversion, which contains all the major building blocks used in a UPS system. We can expand on our black box example from **What is a Static UPS** to gain an understanding of the major components in the double-conversion system.

A double-conversion UPS can be broken down into several smaller black boxes, a rectifier, inverter, static switch, and stored energy device. We will use batteries as our stored energy device because they are the primary source used at the time of this writing. Other technologies are emerging, and they will be discussed briefly in the section **Summary of Other Technologies**.

As with all black boxes, there is an input and output, and each has a specific function.

Rectifier

As we break our UPS system down into these blocks, the first major component we come to is the rectifier. The purpose of all rectifiers is to change AC voltage into DC voltage. This DC voltage is used to support what is commonly called a DC Bus, which is the connection between the rectifier, the stored energy device, and the inverter. (See Figure 4.)

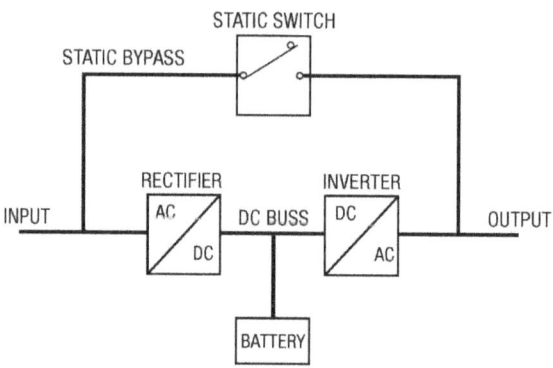

Figure 4

Other names used for rectifiers are battery charger and AC to DC converter. Some models of UPS systems will use a separate battery charger that can be turned off when the batteries are fully charged. It will then monitor the batteries and when they need to be charged it will turn back on. This system helps with cell dry out that leads to reduced life of Valve Regulated Lead Acid batteries, which will be discussed later. For a double-conversion system with separate battery chargers, there needs to be a rectifier to support the DC Bus during normal operation. All UPS systems need a battery charger–a type of rectifier–to keep batteries charged and recharge them after a power outage.

Some rectifier systems use what is called a walk-in circuit. This circuit 'walks' up its output, or the DC Bus, slowly. Walking the DC Bus up gradually accomplishes several useful things, including protecting the DC filter caps and reducing inrush current to the system, which we'll discuss later.

Inverter

Connected to the output of the DC Bus is the inverter. (See Figure 4.) The inverter converts DC power to AC power, which supplies the critical load. An inverter is a rectifier operating backwards and its function is to change DC into AC voltage. All AC UPS systems have an inverter to change the stored DC energy from the rectifier or batteries to AC power.

Energy Storage — Batteries

The third connection to our DC Bus is our stored energy source. A stored energy source provides DC power to the inverter when the normal AC power is not available. This normal AC source could be utility or generator power.

Static Switch

The static switch is the last major component in a traditional double-conversion UPS system. The purpose of the static switch is to provide a method to transfer the critical load from the inverter to a bypass source without interruption. If bypass power is available and acceptable, the system will transfer the load to the bypass source. It's important to understand that bypass power is not UPS protected power. If the input source is lost, the critical load will lose power.

The static switch is critical when a UPS has a failure or maintenance is required.

Short-Term Cost Savings

Unfortunately, cost is often the deciding factor when selecting a UPS system. Many end users think all UPS systems are equal, therefore why not pick the one with the lowest cost? Sometimes the end user does not even get involved, instead leaving it up to the electrical contractor, the landlord or the design firm that may not have a solid understanding of the customer's present and future needs. Eventually, the day comes when the UPS system requires corrective maintenance and the customer is advised he or she must shut down the IT system while repairs are being completed. "What do you mean I have to shut down, I have a UPS!?"

A UPS system, with internal maintenance bypass only, is one such cost-saving design. (See Figure 5.) Internal maintenance bypass is quite common as it reduces the cost of installation. Many systems use an internal maintenance bypass and are sold as having a wrap-around bypass.

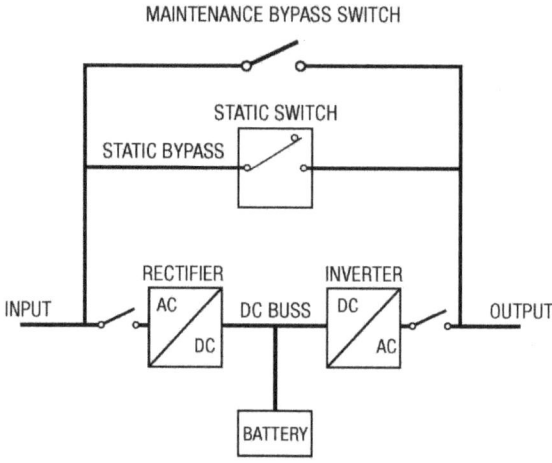

Figure 5

An external maintenance bypass, on the other hand, allows the entire structure of the UPS system to be bypassed. This enables all power to be removed from the "box." In most cases, the entire UPS box could be removed and replaced without losing power to the critical load. (See Figure 6.)

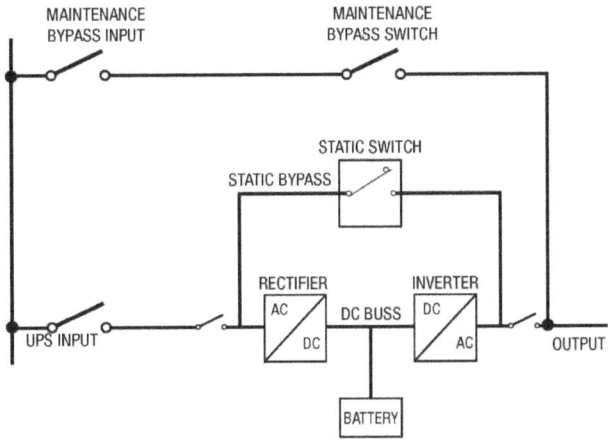

Figure 6

Which type of maintenance bypass system is deployed depends on factors such as cost and need. Service technicians prefer an external bypass system because it allows complete isolation and all maintenance and repairs to be completed safely.

It's also important to understand that many people in the industry will use the term bypass liberally. When deciding on which system to buy, or whether to include a maintenance bypass, you will need to understand what the advantages and disadvantages are for each.

Advantages of an internal maintenance bypass include reduced cost, ease of installation, and space savings.

Major disadvantages include a major failure of the system that could require all power be removed. This means the critical load would need to be shut down, and it would be shut down during the entire repair process.

I have seen many systems in which an internal maintenance bypass did not allow for certain parts to be replaced. The design engineers may have assumed the system would be replaced before those components failed, or perhaps the system was designed to be more cost-conscious. An internal maintenance bypass increases the reliability of a system, but only slightly over having a static switch.

External maintenance bypass is a system that is both electrically and physically external to the rectifier, inverter, and static switch. This allows for the critical load to continue to receive power while the UPS system is undergoing repairs. A key advantage of an external maintenance bypass over the internal maintenance bypass is the ability to isolate both physically and electrically the critical load from the UPS system. One simple way to determine if a bypass is external is to ask a question, "Can the entire UPS system be removed and replaced without powering down the critical load?" If the answer is yes, it's external.

A second cost saving is integrated distribution. (See Figure 7.) It is often used to save money or space, similar to an internal maintenance bypass. Because it is inside or attached to the main UPS unit, there is limited additional floor space required. This also reduces the amount of equipment purchased and the amount of electrical work required, all reducing the cost of installation.

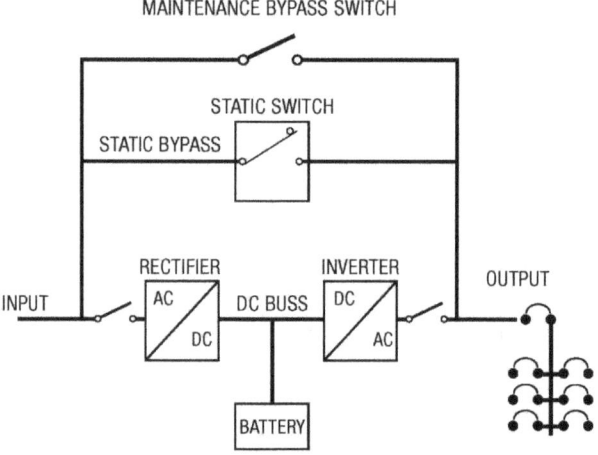

Figure 7

This system works well in certain applications. It's critical that decision-makers are aware of the limitations and understand any long-term impacts to their operations. When there is a failure in the UPS system that requires the input/bypass power to be removed, the load must be shut down to make the repair.

Integrated distribution is typically available on 208/208V or 480/208V input/output units.

3. Operating Modes

To keep things simple, we will start by discussing four operational states of our critical power system:

- Normal Mode – The load is being supported and protected.
- Bypass Mode – The load has power but is not protected.
- Battery Mode – The load is being supported by batteries, likely because of a utility power outage.
- Off – The critical load does not have power.

Sometimes we have no control over operational status. If the UPS system fails, it will go to static bypass. If there is a utility power outage, the system should run on batteries. Planning maintenance gives us control over the date and time. If there is a generator, we can decide if we want to operate from a generator or utility power while performing maintenance.

Normal Mode

For our purposes, normal operation is a condition in which the UPS system has input power and is protecting the critical load against a power loss.

During normal operation of a double-conversion UPS system, power flows from the input source, through the rectifier, across the DC Bus to the inverter. The inverter provides power to the critical load. (See Figure 8.)

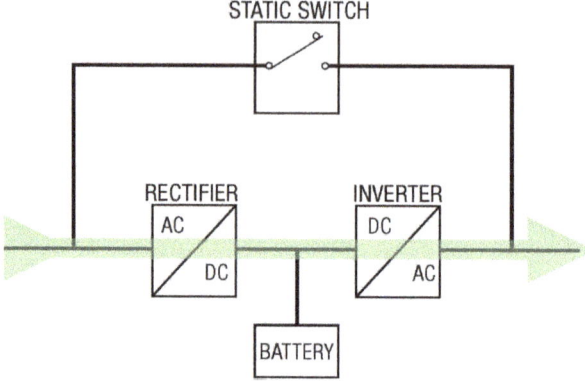

Figure 8

If the batteries are charging, power will also flow from the DC Bus into the batteries. (See Figure 9.)

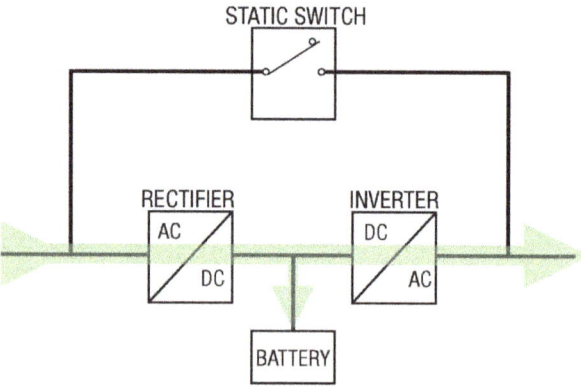

Figure 9

Sometimes you will hear the term "online operation." This term can be misleading in that certain single-conversion UPS systems are in normal operation but are offline. This type of system operates online only when operating from batteries and is discussed in more detail in **UPS Topologies**.

Battery Mode

Battery operation is just what it sounds like—the UPS system is operating on batteries. (See Figure 10.) When the input power fails, power is drawn from the batteries through the DC Bus to the inverter. This is true for all topologies of UPS systems, not just double conversion.

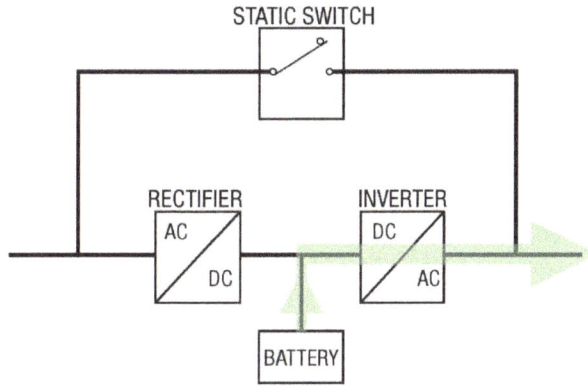

Figure 10

Bypass Mode

There are two types of bypasses, static bypass and maintenance bypass. It's important to remember that when a system is in bypass, the load is not protected. If the input power is lost, the load will lose power.

   Static bypass gets its name from the original UPS systems using a "static switch" to bypass the rectifier and inverter when a fault occurs. This allows the load to continue to operate from unprotected power. The switch is called static because it is an electronic switch that is solid state, not mechanical. The static switch provides a method to bypass the rectifier and inverter when maintenance must be completed without shutting down the load. (See Figure 11.)

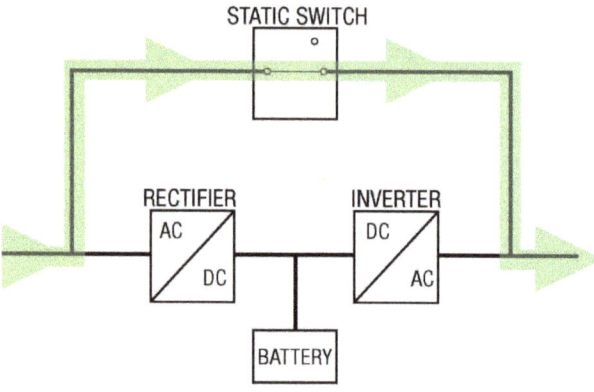

Figure 11

The second type of bypass is maintenance bypass. An in-depth discussion on the types of bypass configurations can be found in the section **Short-Term Cost Savings**.

4. More UPS Components

Hopefully, you have made it this far without falling asleep. The following section will not be any more exciting but is necessary for a full understanding of UPS systems.

The following components can be found to varying degrees in different systems and are discussed in more detail in other sections of this book.

Filters

Merriam Webster defines a filter as a "device or material for suppressing or minimizing waves or oscillations of certain frequencies (as of electricity, light, or sound)." In simple terms, filters remove the parts of a waveform we don't want.

There are two types of filters in modern UPS systems—DC and AC—and they are made up of capacitors and inductors.

Capacitors

Capacitors come in different sizes and shapes. (See Figure 12.) But all capacitors work in essentially the same way.

Figure 12

A capacitor is made of two or more parallel conductive plates, often metal. The plates are separated by an insulating material called a dielectric such as waxed paper, ceramic, or plastic. (See Figure 13.) A capacitor stores energy and opposes a change in voltage.

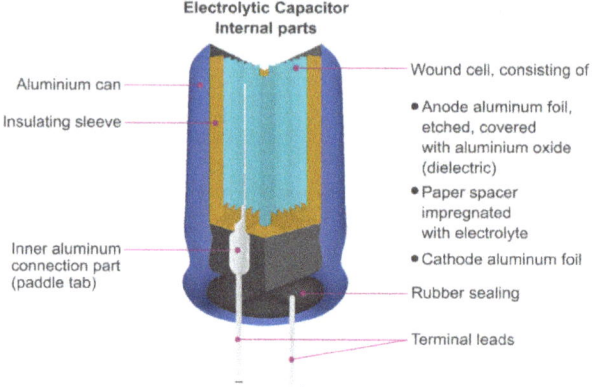

Figure 13

Inductors

An inductor is a coil of wire that stores energy in a magnetic field and opposes a change in current. (See Figure 14.)

Figure 14

DC Filters

When the AC power is rectified by the semiconductors, it creates a waveform that looks similar to Figure 15. To lessen the valleys and form a smoother DC voltage, DC filters are used. Once a capacitor is installed, we will get a voltage that looks more like a straight line or direct current as in Figure 16.

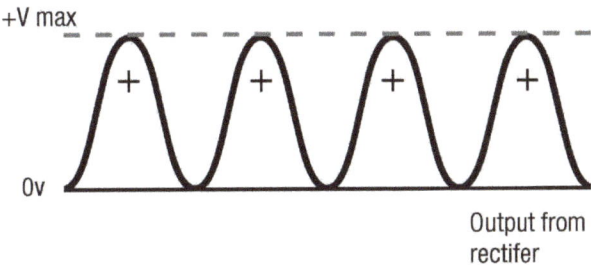

Figure 15

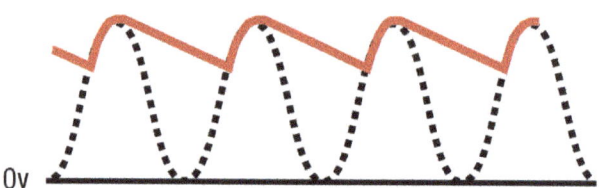

Figure 16

All UPS systems will have a DC filter of varying degrees. However, the larger the rectifier, the larger the DC filter will need to be. UPS systems with only small battery chargers will have small DC filters.

AC Filters

While DC filters are made up primarily of capacitors, AC filters contain both capacitors and inductors, often called chokes. The configuration of these components forms what are dubbed traps because they "trap" unwanted parts of a waveform known as distortion.

Input Filters

When AC voltage is rectified, it often causes current harmonics to be reflected back toward the source, resulting in voltage distortion. (See Figure 17.) This distortion can create problems with other loads powered from the same source as the UPS system. To help alleviate this problem, some manufacturers have fitted UPS systems with input filters.

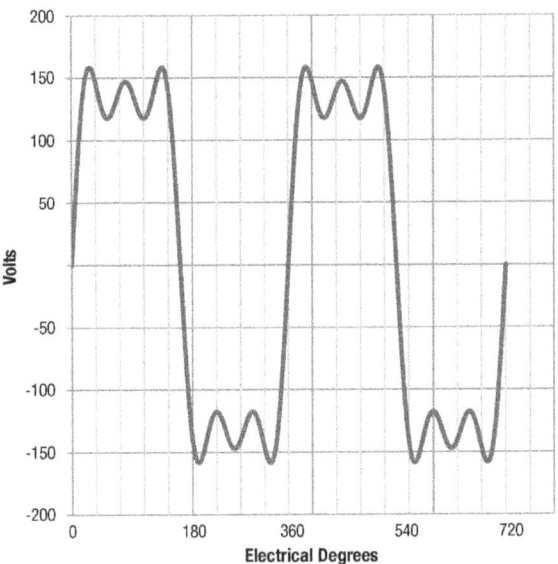

Figure 17

Output Filters

Output filters are used in most modern UPS units to "convert" the pulse width modulated waveform into a sine wave. The filters remove the pulses, making the waveform sinusoidal as shown in Figure 18.

If there is a problem with an output filter, the sine wave could become distorted and passed directly to the load equipment. Sometimes this will damage the equipment.

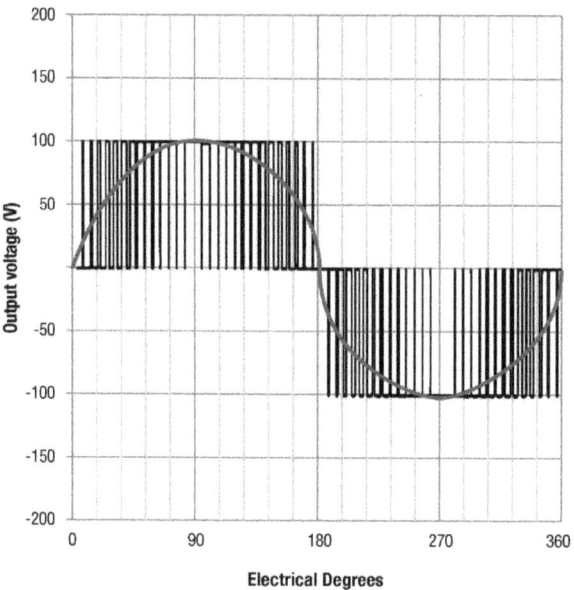

Figure 18

Generators and Filters

Something interesting often happens when engineers try to solve a problem; they create a new one.

From our discussion on UPS Filters, we know that some rectifiers reflect harmonics onto the source. These harmonics can cause issues with other equipment on the same electrical feed. If the harmonic distortion is large enough, the customer causing the distortion can be penalized. Input filters made up of capacitors and inductors are used to remove this distortion.

A UPS system loaded to fifty percent or higher will offset much of the capacitance seen by the source, but a lightly loaded system will not. It's important to note that the rectifier is the load seen by the input filter. When a double-conversion UPS system loses input power, its rectifier shuts off, removing the load from the input filter until the rectifier restarts. This in turn raises the capacitance seen by the source.

Modern rectifiers have a walk-in circuit. After power is reapplied to the rectifier, it takes a certain amount of time for it to turn back on. During this walk-in there is no load on the input filter, resulting in high capacitance seen by the source.

There are several reasons to install these walk-in circuits. The primary reason is to slowly charge the DC caps, eliminating the inrush that occurs when power is first applied. It also allows power to be added slowly to the source, which is important when adding large loads to generators.

A utility source is what we refer to as "stiff," meaning it's large and has a low AC resistance, known as impedance. Fundamentally, it takes a substantial amount of load to change its voltage or frequency. Generators typically have a higher impedance, or a "soft source." This simply means it's much easier to change the voltage waveform compared to a stiffer source such as the utility.

Generators by their nature don't like large capacitive loads, which an input filter is. It causes regulation problems and if it's too capacitive, it will damage the alternator, the part of the generator that produces electric power.

Some UPS manufacturers install contactors, a form of automatic circuit breaker that can disconnect the input filters when the load is low and would cause problems for the generator. (See Figure 19.)

These problems routinely occur when the generator and UPS systems are sized close together, or when there is no other load on the generator to naturally filter out this high capacitance.

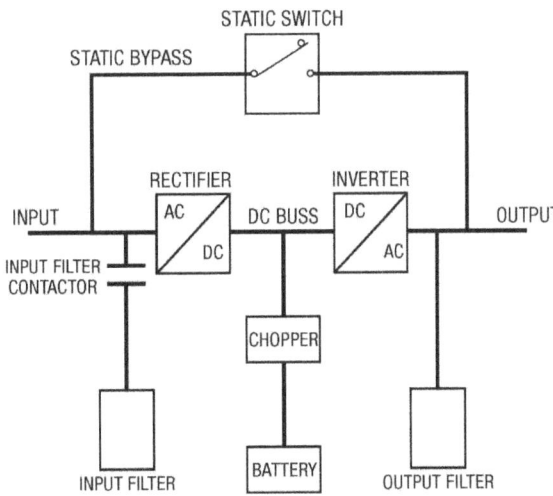

Figure 19

Choppers

Modern UPS systems employ an additional component called a "chopper." A chopper is an electronic DC transformer, or more accurately a DC to DC converter. It is located between the battery bus and the DC Bus. (See Figure 20.)

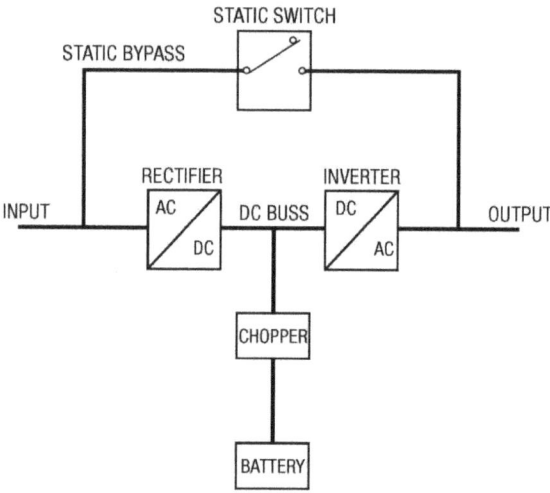

Figure 20

When charging batteries, the chopper reduces the DC voltage from the DC Bus to the float voltage. When batteries are supporting the inverter, it increases the voltage to the DC Bus level.

Manufacturers want the DC voltage as high as safely possible to increase inverter efficiency, but keeping the battery voltage low has several advantages. Batteries are expensive and replacing them every three to five years adds up. The fewer that are needed, the less expensive it will be.

Also, anything above six hundred volts is considered medium voltage by the National Electrical Code (NEC) and must comply with more stringent rules.

Controls and Front Panel

At some point, we'll need to know the status of our UPS system. We will also need to operate it to perform maintenance or to restart it after it fails. (See Figure 21.) Although commonly referred to as the front panel, it would be more accurately described as the user interface.

Figure 21

The primary function of the front panel is to communicate to the user the status of the UPS system and to operate it when needed. As UPS systems have evolved, so have the front panels. Every manufacturer offers a different display and amount of information displayed. Within the same manufacturer, and often between the same models of systems, the displays can be different. But the primary function is the same—a way to operate the system and to tell the operator what is going on.

This normally includes system status. Is the system online and supporting the load, is it in bypass mode, or is it off? It should also display any active alarms and newer systems should include a history of events.

As with all equipment, UPS systems come with operator guides and manuals. Anyone who needs to operate the UPS should become familiar with the operator's guide. It is also helpful to include printed instructions with diagrams on the unit itself. Putting the service company's phone number on the unit, along with a model and serial number, can be invaluable when there is an emergency and the stress level is high.

Communications

All modern UPS systems should be able to interface with a building monitoring system or building management system. Most will also allow users to access them via a network connection.

A word of caution: when purchasing a UPS system, the end user should know how he or she wants to monitor it, then make sure the system is capable of that monitoring and that it is included in the purchase. We often see monitoring discussed *after* the purchase has been made, many times with the startup technician. The end user is upset because it was not included in the sale, and the sales rep is frustrated because it was not specified before the sale was made.

Worse is when communications were purchased but are not compatible with the monitoring service the customer is using. As monitoring becomes more available and necessary, this needs to be discussed in detail when purchasing any equipment, not just UPS systems.

5. UPS System Voltage Options

Before going further, we need a basic understanding of how mechanical power is converted into electrical power.

It all starts with a generator, a device that converts mechanical energy into electrical energy. An engine rotates a magnetic field through a coil creating an electrical potential we call voltage.

It's helpful to visualize AC electrical power as a sinusoidal waveform traveling through 360 degrees. In three-phase, there are three waveforms, each separated by 120 degrees as seen in Figure 22. In single-phase, there can be one or two, as we will discuss soon.

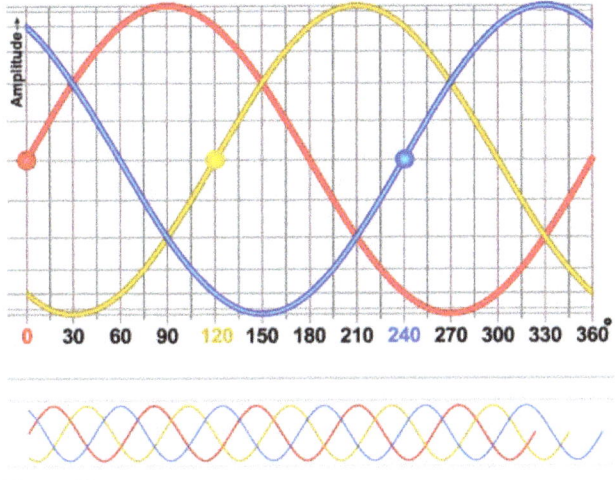

Figure 22

Three-Phase Power

The United States primarily uses two three-phase power configurations when working with UPS systems, 277/480 volts, and 120/208 volts. These are typically used with systems larger than 10kVA.

The higher the voltage, the more efficient and cost-effective it is to distribute. However, most IT equipment cannot use three-phase 480 volts. Therefore, a transformer is needed to step the voltage down to a usable level.

For the U.S., this is typically 120/208 volts, which can then be distributed and used as a single-phase by the critical load equipment.

Single-Phase Voltage

Although it is used for smaller systems, single-phase can be more complicated than three-phase. The different options and terminology can confuse people who do not spend all their time in the industry. This misunderstanding can lead to the purchase of an incorrect UPS system.

Often, this is not noticed until the startup technician arrives and begins performing checks. At this juncture, a different UPS system will need to be purchased, or the electrical installation will need to be corrected. Either option is expensive.

The better everyone's understanding is before buying the system, the smoother the installation and startup will be.

Single-Phase 120-Volt

Single-phase power is distributed on two current-carrying conductors. The voltage waveform is seen in Figure 23. The simplest version is the single-phase 120-volt found in virtually every household in the United States. Any load that plugs into a standard wall outlet is a single-phase 120-volt load, which includes common household items such as lamps, TVs, and toasters.

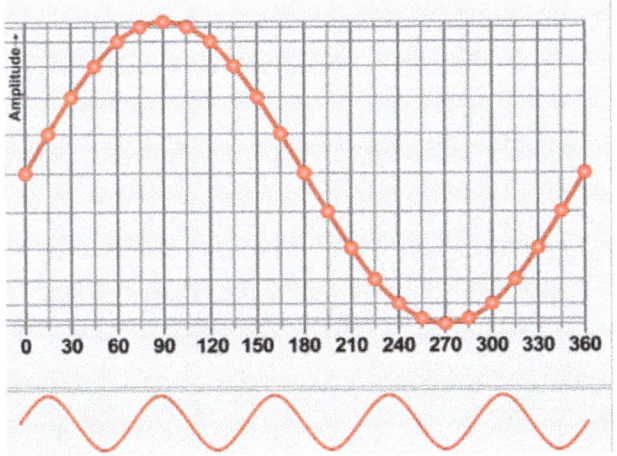

Figure 23

Single-phase 120-volt UPS systems are single point of use devices. They plug into the wall and then your computer, for example, plugs into the UPS system. They are often found under desks supporting individual workstations. (See Figure 24.)

Figure 24

Split-Phase

Split-phase power, sometimes called two-phase or dual-phase, is derived from a center-tapped transformer and has one phase of 240-volt power and two phases of 120-volt power. Large household appliances such as clothes dryers, water heaters, HVAC and kitchen stoves use 240-volt single-phase power, while small appliances that plug into wall outlets, such as toasters, microwave ovens, mixers, and desk lamps use 120-volt single-phase.

In split-phase power, the relationship between the waveforms can become a little more complicated. In our homes, we have split-phase 240 and the waveforms are separated by 180 degrees. With this configuration we get 120 volts or 240 volts. (See Figure 25.)

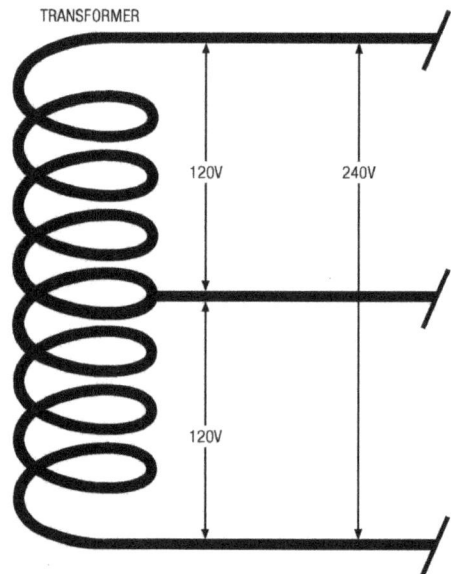

Figure 25

We can also get split phase 208 by using two of the three phases of three-phase power. Here however, the two 120-volt sources are separated by 120 degrees.

The key here is to understand what your needs are and what the UPS system is capable of supplying. Many modern IT loads can work from either

208- or 240-volt, but if you have loads that require 120-volt, care must be taken when selecting a UPS system.

One problem involves systems that will provide 208-volt split-phase or 240 split-phase with a 120 option. But you cannot use the 208 split-phase and get 120 volts line to neutral. You will get 120 volts on phase to ground and 80 volts on the other. (See Figure 26.)

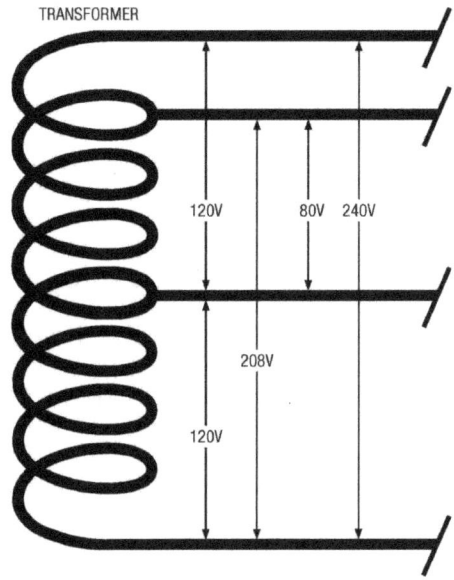

Figure 26

To save costs, the transformer inside the unit is wired such that it provides both 240/120-volt and 208/120-volt.

These are usually smaller units that are cost-effective to purchase and work well in many applications. As always, the system being purchased must work in your applications.

6. Control Logic Circuits

While the UPS control logic has many functions, two of the main ones are to protect the critical load and protect itself. Each system will accomplish this differently. But if we keep these functions in mind, we can often work through why the system did what it did.

Because these systems are complex and different from model to model, we will only discuss major alarms, what causes them, and what it means for the load.

The first function of a UPS system is to protect the critical load from power problems, most often an outage. That's it. If it can't do that, it is not doing its job.

Additionally, output under voltage can cause equipment to mis-operate or shut down, and over voltages can cause damage to load equipment. Output frequency deviations can cause equipment to fail. Logic must monitor for these failures and transfer the load to a safe source or shut down if they occur.

Also, if the DC voltage is too low, the inverter will not produce the correct AC voltage. There is a circuit that shuts off the inverter when the DC voltage falls to a certain level. This low DC voltage shutoff also protects the batteries from being discharged to a level that permanently damages them. If the DC voltage is too high, it can damage the batteries, cause DC filter capacitors to fail and even damage the inverter.

When a failure occurs with the UPS unit, the system checks to be sure the bypass source is acceptable, and if so, automatically transfers the load to it. The load will not be protected, but neither will it be exposed to the potential damage of a malfunctioning inverter.

If the bypass source is not available or is unacceptable, the UPS system will shut down.

The most common alarms are explained in Table 1. It includes the reasons why the condition could occur and what the system will do. Keep in mind this is general and different systems will do these things at different times and in distinct ways.

Table 1

Typical Alarm	Condition/Description	Typical UPS Response
DC Undervoltage (DCUV) Low Battery Shutdown	DC Bus voltage level has decreased to a level that will cause permeant damage to the batteries or the inverter will not be able to make nominal voltage.	UPS system shuts down opening input CB, battery CB, and output CB. Load will be transferred to bypass if acceptable. DCUV alarms normally occur because of a utility power outage.
DC Overvoltage (DCOV)	DC Bus voltage has increased to a level that will cause damage to the filter caps and batteries.	UPS Shuts down opening input CB, battery CB, and output CB. Load will be transferred to bypass if acceptable.
Output Overvoltage (ACOV)	Inverter output voltage has increased to a level that his dangerous the load and UPS system.	UPS shuts down, opening input CB, battery CB, and output CB. Load will be transferred to bypass if acceptable.
Output Undervoltage (ACUV)	Inverter output voltage has decreased to a level that will not support the load.	UPS shuts down opening input CB, battery CB, and output CB. Load will be transferred to bypass if acceptable.
Bypass Sync (Non Sync)	The bypass voltage and inverter voltage are no longer in sync. A no-break transfer is not possible.	UPS will free run, its output frequency set by its internal logic. If there is a failure of the UPS while free running, it will shut down by opening its battery CB, Input CB, and output CB. Some systems will transfer to bypass but with a several-second loss of power to the load. Other systems will not.
Low Battery Warning	DC Bus decreased to a specific level indicating a DCUV is imminent.	The system produces an alarm. No other action.
On Battery	The inverter of the UPS system is operating from battery, normally as a result of an input power outage.	The system produces an alarm and continues to support the critical load.
Input/Mains Failure	The input power to the UPS is no longer available, likely due to a power outage.	The system will alarm and operate on batteries until input power has returned or DCUV.
Bypass Unavailable or Bypass Out of Tolerance	The bypass voltage or frequency is not acceptable to support the load.	UPS system breaks sync and will free run if possible or operate on batteries if line interactive.
Summary Alarm	A general alarm often used to notify a user that the UPS has changed status.	This is alarm is secondary to a primary alarm. The primary alarm would determine what the UPS system will do.

Control Logic Circuits | 35

Over Load	Load has increased to a level that the UPS can no longer support.	Each UPS system has an overload percentage set point. It will continue to protect the load up to this point before transferring to bypass.
Over Temperature	The internal temperature of the system has exceeded its operation limit.	System will transfer to bypass and shut down.
Fan Failure	A fan has failed inside the unit.	Some units will continue to operate giving an alarm. Others will transfer to bypass and shutdown.

Often there will be several alarms for the same status change. An example would be when the input power to the UPS system is lost. On many systems, the input and bypass power are from the same source. If one is missing, the other will also be missing.

The UPS system monitors many parameters of the input and bypass power and will trigger an alarm when any of them are outside acceptable limits. If the power is completely gone, the voltage and frequency of both the input and bypass sources are out of tolerance. This will cause the following alarms:

- Input Voltage Out of Tolerance.
- Input Frequency Out of Tolerance.
- Bypass Voltage Out of Tolerance.
- Bypass Frequency Out of Tolerance.
- Non-Sync Alarm (there is no bypass source to synchronize to).

The UPS system operator's manual should have a list of alarms, what each means, and which steps to take next if needed.

7. UPS Topologies

What is UPS topology? What does it mean for you and why should you care?

Topology can be defined as the configuration of a UPS system unit. We are speaking specifically of a single module. This differs from the UPS system's configuration as it relates to multi-module configurations. The topology or configuration is the makeup of the UPS system, in other words, which building blocks make up the unit.

To maintain conformity, the Institute of Electrical and Electronics Engineers (IEEE) Standard 446-1995, "Recommended Practice for Emergency and Standby Power Systems for Industrial and Commercial Applications," was used as much as possible to identify and define the types of UPS topologies.

Manufacturers refer to different systems with terms other than those defined by IEEE, but these are marketing techniques, and at the end of the day all can be identified using one of the IEEE definitions.

IEEE Standard 446-1995 defines two categories of UPS topologies: double conversion and single conversion. It defines several other subcategories of the single-conversion UPS system:

- Line Interactive
- Tri-port
- Ferroresonant

Each topology will protect against power problems in distinct ways. The level of protection and criticality of your load will influence what type of topology you want.

Online vs. Offline

A quick note about online vs. offline UPS systems: the IEEE does not define online or offline UPS systems. These labels are used by the industry and manufacturers to promote or better understand the various products.

Double-conversion UPS topology would once have always been considered an online system. But with today's eco and standby modes, double-conversion systems can now be labeled offline, depending on their mode of operation.

Several line-interactive UPS topologies are online systems, but they are not double-conversion. Many engineers and facility personnel don't like the term line-interactive, so the terms online and offline were coined.

Double Conversion

One of the original UPS system designs was the double-conversion system, which uses all the major components discussed in Major Components. (See Figure 27.)

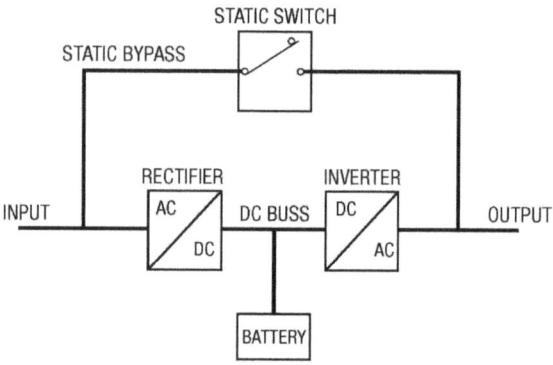

Figure 27

This topology uses a rectifier to change incoming AC voltage into DC voltage. This DC voltage is then used to charge the batteries and supply power to the inverter. The inverter in turn changes DC voltage to AC voltage, which is supplied to the load.

Conversion of AC to DC and back to AC requires two conversions, thus the name double-conversion.

A common question or concern is how long the break in power is between the incoming power failure and the UPS system operation from batteries. For a double-conversion UPS system, this break is nonexistent. In other topologies, there can be a momentary break of several milliseconds.

Eco Mode

With the current climate of increasing efficiency and decreasing overall total cost of ownership, several manufacturers have added a new mode of operation to the double-conversion UPS system. The mode is often called eco mode, just as in newer automobiles. Each manufacturer has a unique name, and each accomplishes it differently, but the result is the same—the rectifier and inverter are "phased back" and utility power is passed directly to the load, typically through the static switch. Phased back means the power components are on and ready to work at a moment's notice, but they are not doing any work. Like an electric car at a stoplight, the engine is not running, but as soon as you press on the gas it springs into action.

If the system senses a problem with the input power, it will instantly phase on the inverter to support the critical load. The batteries will be charged by either a separate charger or the rectifier will be phased on every so often.

Eco mode eliminates the losses of a loaded rectifier and inverter, allowing some of these UPS systems to achieve ninety-nine percent efficiency.

Single Conversion

There are several types of single conversion systems and these are sometimes referred to as "line-interactive." Line-interactive systems are a form of single conversion, but not all single conversion systems are line-interactive.

The major difference between a single conversion and double-conversion system is that single conversion does not require all of the incoming AC voltage to be converted to DC. During normal operation, these systems provide power to the critical load through a combination of components to produce an impedance. These components include transformers, inductors, and capacitors, depending on the topology and the manufacturer.

A single conversion system uses an inverter to convert the battery power to AC when a problem is sensed with the input power.

There is a battery charger that keeps the batteries charged during normal operation and recharges them after a power outage. Sometimes a single conversion system's charger is not large enough to support the inverter.

Line-interactive

A line-interactive UPS system is a form of single conversion.

The inverter "interacts" with the line power through the use of transformers and inductors to buck or boost the voltage to the critical load. This same inverter is then used during a complete input power outage to supply power to the critical load using the batteries to power the inverter. (See Figure 28.)

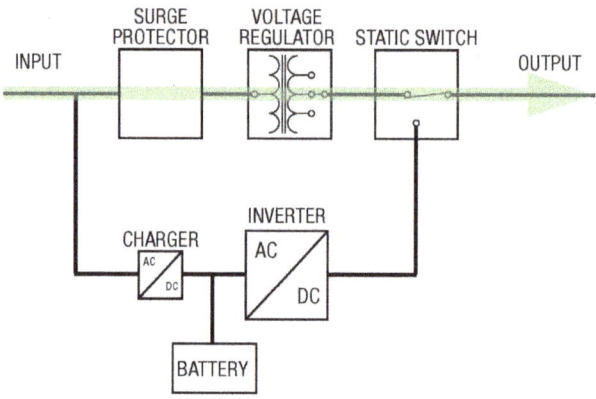

Figure 28

A significant limitation of a line-interactive UPS system is its inability to free run without using batteries. If the frequency of the input voltage is not within the UPS system's program window of operation, it uses its batteries to operate the inverter. When the batteries have become exhausted, it will shut down on DCUV, even if input power is available.

This normally happens when operating on a generator. The generator frequency will fluctuate from nominal by more than the UPS will handle. This can happen when a large load like a motor or air conditioning system is abruptly applied to the generator.

A UPS system could have its frequency window set for sixty HZ +- one percent, meaning the input to the UPS must be between 59.4 and 60.6 HZ. If the frequency is outside that window, the UPS must run on batteries to keep its output frequency within that window. In this instance, we will get a call from a customer that their UPS has shut down and dropped the load. But the generator is running, causing a great deal of confusion and frustration.

To correct this issue, the input voltage frequency window would need to be opened, often to three percent or even five percent when experiencing this problem. This allows the UPS to stay synced with the generator and not use the batteries.

The load will be exposed to the frequency variation. Today's loads are not as frequency-sensitive as older ones, but this needs to be verified before the change is made.

Other options are to increase the size of the generator or remove the loads causing the frequency deviation. These can be cost-prohibitive or feasibly impossible.

Tri-port

The name tri-port comes from the fact that the input, inverter, and load all share the same transformer core, forming three ports. (See Figure 29.) This allows for correction of any input voltage deviations, but because the inverter is in parallel with the main input voltage, it need not support the entire load. This increases efficiencies considerably.

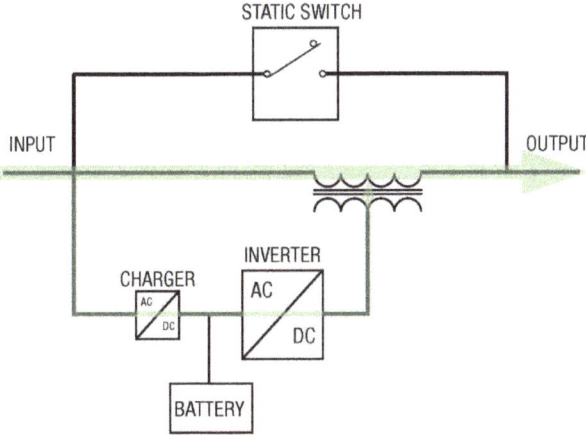

Figure 29

The inverter can be configured to act as a battery charger during normal operation or a separate charger can be used.

Because the inverter often runs constantly, this topology is considered online. However, it is not double conversion because it interacts with the input line voltage, making it a line-interactive UPS system.

The tri-port UPS system has the same limitation as a line-interactive UPS system—its inability to free run without using batteries.

Ferroresonant

A ferroresonant UPS unit is one that uses a special transformer called a ferroresonant. Most transformers operate in a specific voltage window allowing for the highest efficiency; a ferroresonant transformer is designed to operate fully saturated. This reduces efficiency but allows for a very stable voltage and frequency output.

Using a combination of a ferroresonant transformer and capacitors, a tank circuit is created that stores energy. (See Figure 30.) This energy is then used during an outage until the inverter can start and support the load from batteries. Tank circuits have several electrical cycles of power, just long enough for the inverter to start.

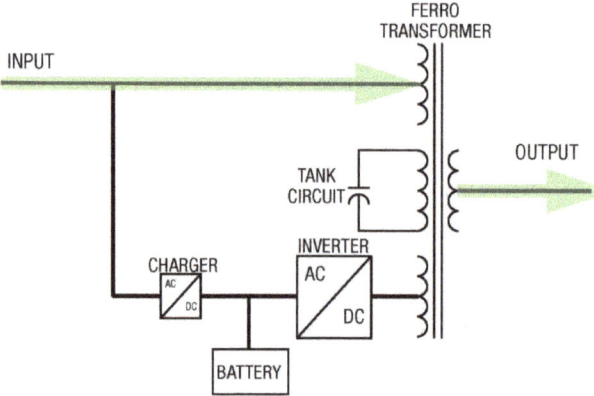

Figure 30

The ferroresonant transformer provides for line condition, noise isolation, and voltage regulation because it is operated in the saturation region. Efficiencies are low for a modern UPS system and are not generally used in data centers or network closets. Because of how robust they are, some are still used in certain industrial applications.

Choosing the Correct Topology

Which product to buy—the most expensive, the highest-rated, the cheapest? All of us struggle with these questions in our personal purchases and our businesses.

About the same time I started in the UPS business, a new product was released in the U.S. called the Silcon. It was marketed as Delta Conversion, which the IEEE defines as a tri-port system, and it enjoyed tremendous success in the market. Priced below much of the competition and sold by APC, it took the market by storm. APC was well known in the IT marketplace for its small, single-phase systems and had a loyal following of IT professionals. APC marketed this three-phase product to these loyal customers when the market was doing well and companies had the capital to purchase the needed UPS systems.

From the beginning, several problems indicated the Silcon UPS was not the Cadillac of the industry. A coworker of mine hated the system and criticized it at every opportunity; it was junk. I was young and respected this worker's opinion with very little questioning. He had more experience in the UPS industry.

There was one major problem with this theory—customers bought them. A lot of them. During my first few years, I spent half my working hours starting Silcon units and completing preventive maintenance and corrective services—much more than any other product.

Why did customers love them, and maybe more important, why did technicians and many engineers hate them?

They got the job done ninety percent of the time. They were inexpensive to buy and repair, easy to purchase and easy to install. From the IT manager's perspective, the "perfect" solution to their problem, cheap UPS backup.

I own a Honda CRV that works great for eighty percent of my purposes and gets great gas mileage. It fits into the ever-shrinking parking spots and parking garages and has plenty of room for our family trips to the beach. However, it is not well-suited for work on the family farm; for that we need a pick-up truck. As much as I would like a new one, the amount of times we need it doesn't justify it. My fifteen-year-old Ford F150 fits our budget and matches our needs better.

The Silcon UPS system fit many customers' budgets and matched their needs during its heyday in the early 21st century.

What my coworker failed to understand, is not every customer needed the most reliable, most robust UPS system on the market. Many needed a quick, easy, inexpensive solution to provide battery backup for major power abnormalities.

The point of this story is not to sell a Silcon UPS system. The manufacturer of the Silcon stopped selling it in 2005. My point is everyone's purpose for a UPS System is different, just as everyone's budget and need for a vehicle are different. What works for my company will not work well for someone else.

We see installations where the UPS system is not a great fit. The end user needs more reliability than the system can provide. This is why the purpose of the UPS System must be defined and the proper system installed to match.

There is no right or wrong system, just the one that best fits your application and budget. Knowing the advantages and disadvantages of each of the UPS topologies is important when deciding which one to purchase. An honest look at what the risks are and performing a cost-benefit analysis is critical. This will take more time and research upfront but will save money and heartache later.

8. Power Problems

As we have discussed before, the primary job of a UPS system is to provide uninterrupted power to the critical load. Before we can understand how the different UPS system topologies will help with power problems, we need to know what those power problems are.

You will hear many terms, and each person could mean something different when discussing them. We will use the terms defined by IEEE Standard 1159-2009 to be sure we are speaking the same language. I recommend that when you discuss power problems with other professionals, you use these terms.

This is a brief explanation of power quality terms and is not intended to describe how these problems are created or offer solutions. Please refer to the appendix for resources to better understand power problems.

Something to keep in mind when we discuss how UPS systems handle power problems: we are talking about the problems on the input to the UPS system. Unless the UPS system is broken, any power problems on the output of the UPS system are caused by the load equipment. The UPS topology, manufacturer, and model will impact how these problems are handled.

The UPS system cannot correct the problem, it can only continue to support the load.

Defining Power Problems

According to IEEE Standard 1159-2009, "Recommended Practice for Monitoring Electric Power Quality," there are seven types of power quality problems:

- Interruptions
- Sag/Undervoltage
- Swell/Overvoltage
- Waveform Distortion
- Voltage Fluctuations
- Transients
- Frequency Variations

We will define each problem in more detail.

- Interruptions – An interruption is a complete loss of power. There are four categories of interruptions.

    - <u>Instantaneous</u> – This interruption lasts from 0.5 to thirty cycles, 8ms to 500ms (half a second). Often, we will not notice an instantaneous outage with current technologies. Our clocks will not reset, and lights may not flicker. However, critical computer equipment can shut down or mis-operate.
    - <u>Momentary</u> – This interruption lasts from thirty cycles (half a second) to two seconds. This interruption will cause lights to flicker and clocks may reset. Even the most technologically advanced equipment will shut down. Often you will hear this referred to as a power bump or blip.
    - <u>Temporary</u> – Temporary interruptions last from two seconds to two minutes.
    - <u>Sustained</u> – Sustained interruptions are anything longer than two minutes and are what most of us would consider a power outage or blackout.

    All UPS systems should correct for interruptions by operating from batteries.

- Sag/Undervoltage – Sags and undervoltage are both a reduction in voltage from nominal by five percent. As an example, in our homes, the voltage would drop below 114 volts.

    Sags last from 0.5 cycle, 8ms to one minute, where an undervoltage would be a reduction in voltage for more than one minute. We often have no way of noticing a sag or undervoltage without special equipment.

    Brownouts are sometimes used to describe sag and undervoltage events. However, brownouts are a specific strategy used by power companies to help reduce high power demand usage and they can result in an undervoltage condition. Brownouts are not defined by the IEEE as a power quality problem, but they can be problems for critical load equipment. All UPS systems should help with a sag or undervoltage by maintaining a constant voltage to the load.

- Swell/Overvoltage – Swells and overvoltages are the opposite of sags and undervoltages. They are an increase in voltage above normal by five percent. Swells last from 0.5 cycles to one minute and overvoltages are anything over a minute. For your typical household, this would be an increase in voltage over six volts, or above 126 volts. Again, without special equipment, it is very difficult to notice this increase in voltage.

    All UPS systems should help with swells and overvoltage by maintaining a constant voltage to the load.

- Waveform Distortion – There are five types of waveform distortions.
    - DC Offset – Direct current offset is when the voltage waveform is still a sine wave, but the waveform has moved above or below its correct zero-crossing.
    - Harmonics – Harmonic distortion is when the fundamental waveform is distorted from its sinusoidal form. This is the result of something in the power system causing additional waveforms at a frequency that is a multiple of the fundamental, i.e. 180 would be 3 x 60.
    - Inter-harmonics – These are harmonics that are not an integer of the fundamental, something like 90 Hz, or 1.5X 60Hz.
    - Notching – Notching is a periodic disturbance on the waveform.
    - Noise – Noise is an unwanted voltage or current imposed on the fundamental waveform.

- Voltage fluctuations – Voltage fluctuations are defined by IEEE Standard 1159-2009 as "systematic variations of the voltage envelope or a series of random voltage changes, the magnitude of which does not normally exceed the voltage ranges of 0.95 to 1.05 Pu."

    In simple terms, a voltage fluctuation is a variation in the voltage from its nominal down to ninety-five percent and up to 105 percent. In a 120-volt system, this would be a change from 120 volts down to 114 volts and up to 126 volts. Anything greater than this change would be a sag/undervoltage event or a swell/overvoltage event.
    Each UPS topology will handle this differently.

- Transients – Transients come in two categories, impulsive and oscillatory. IEEE Standard 1159-2009 defines an impulsive transient as "a sudden, non-power frequency change in the steady-state condition of voltage, current or both, that is unidirectional in polarity." This means there is a spike on the waveform in one direction.

Lightning is the most common cause of impulsive transients. Oscillatory transients are voltage or current whose instantaneous value changes polarity rapidly, in both directions. The difference between impulsive and oscillatory is impulsive happens one time on the waveform where oscillatory repeats on the waveform.

- Frequency variations – As the name implies, a frequency variation is when the frequency deviates from its fundamental. In most developed countries, frequency variations are uncommon while operating from utility power. They can occur while operating on a small generator or when a large load is applied to a generator.

    Some UPS topologies handle frequency variations by operation on batteries. This means even though there is input power to the UPS system it will run on batteries, and when they are exhausted the system will shut down. All other equipment on the generator will continue to operate, causing confusion and frustration.

    See Table 2 for information on how each topology corrects for frequency variations.

Table 2

Types of Power Problems (Input to the UPS System)	How They are Corrected			
	Double Conversion	Line Interactive	Tri-port	Ferroresonant
Interruptions	The inverter of the double-conversion UPS system will continue to draw power from the DC Bus. It will not know that the input has been interrupted. But the DC Bus will begin to draw its power from the batteries. Often you will hear someone ask how long it takes the UPS to switch to batteries. In a double-conversion system, there is no switch or break.	There is an outage of approximately twenty milliseconds while the inverter starts. After the inverter starts the system works as all others, the batteries support the inverter until input power returns or the batteries are exhausted and the system shuts down. This short outage does not affect most modern loads.	The inverter is always running in a tri-port system. When the input power fails, the inverter will draw power from the batteries instead of the utility. The batteries will continue to support the inverter until the power returns, or the batteries are exhausted.	The tank circuit will support the load until the inverter starts. Energy from the batteries will be used by the inverter until power returns or the batteries are exhausted and the system shuts down.

Sag/Undervoltage & Swell/Overvoltage	The rectifier of a double conversion UPS System is a constant power device. This means when the voltage decreases, the current increases, providing a steady DC voltage to the inverter. The system does not need to do anything for this to happen.	A line-interactive UPS system will have an adjustable setting to handle input voltage ranges. If the voltage is within this tolerance, it will pass it directly to the load. If outside this tolerance, it will use the inverter to boost (raise) the voltage to the appropriate level. If the input voltage decreases to a level the system can longer boost to the correct level, it will operate on batteries until the voltage is corrected or the batteries are exhausted.	The inverter is in parallel with the input voltage and interacts with it to raise or lower the voltages as necessary. If there is a sag, it will boost the voltage and if there is a swell it will buck the voltage, much like a line-interactive UPS system. If the input voltage becomes too low or high, the system will operate from batteries until the input returns to normal or the batteries are exhausted.	The ferroresonant transformer operates saturated, providing for inherent voltage regulation for both sags and swells. If the voltage falls outside UPS design setpoints, it will operate from batteries until input power returns to normal or the batteries are exhausted.

Waveform Distortion	Each UPS model will have a specification or tolerance that it can operate from. If the distortion is within this tolerance, the rectifier will convert the distorted waveform to a DC voltage, which removes the distortion due to its inherent physical properties. If the distortion is outside the UPS system's tolerance window, it can disconnect from the input source and operate on batteries until the source is back in tolerance.	The input noise/surge filter will remove any distortion it is able to. The remainder will be passed along to the load, or if the system senses the issue, it will operate from batteries until the problem is corrected or the batteries are exhausted.	Using the input impedance–the inverter–the system will correct for the distortion if possible. If it is unable to correct for it, the system will either pass the remainder of the distortion on to the load or operate from batteries.	The ferroresonant transformer will block or correct any distortion it is able to, and the rest will be passed along to the load. If the system detects the problem, it could operate from batteries until the issue is corrected or the batteries are exhausted.

Voltage Fluctuations	Because the rectifier of a double-conversion UPS system converts all incoming AC power to DC; this small change in voltage will be converted to DC and provided to the inverter. No change in the operation of the UPS system is required and the fluctuation will not be passed to the load.	A line-interactive UPS system will have an adjustable setting to handle input voltage ranges. If the voltage is within this tolerance, it will pass it directly to the load. If outside this tolerance, it will use the inverter to buck (lower) or boost (raise) the voltage to the appropriate level.	The inverter of a tri-port system is always running and making adjustments to the input power. Any voltage fluctuation on the utility will be corrected by this operation, providing regulated power to the load.	The ferroresonant transformer operates saturated, providing for inherent voltage regulation. The inherent properties of a ferroresonant transformer provide regulation for voltage fluctuations with no need to change its operating condition.
Transients	The rectifier of a double-conversion UPS system converts all incoming AC power to DC; this small change in voltage will be converted to DC and provided to the inverter. It will not be passed directly to the load.	The input of a line-interactive UPS system is equipped with a noise/surge protector; this is designed to block transients.	The input to a tri-port system consists of an impedance in series with the input power, often an inductor. This impedance will block transients from the load.	Because a ferroresonant transformer operates completely saturated, it will block transients to the load.

9. Misunderstood Concepts

During my career I have noticed certain concepts of UPS systems misunderstood time and again. I have tried to explain many of the them throughout the sections that apply directly to these misunderstandings. But several can't be put into neat boxes. I discuss them here in the hope of helping everyone communicate in the same language.

Efficiency

Merriam-Webster defines efficiency as "the ratio of the useful energy delivered by a dynamic system to the energy supplied to it." For a UPS system, that essentially means it's a percentage of the input power used by the load. An example would be if a UPS system has 80kW of load, and it is ninety percent efficient, it would require approximately 90kW of input power. The remaining 10kW would be lost as heat.

These losses will need to be paid for in electrical costs and larger infrastructure. This infrastructure includes larger electrical feed circuits to the UPS system and additional air conditioning to remove the added heat.

There will always be efficiency losses; we can't make anything one hundred percent efficient, but the lower the losses, or higher the efficiency, the greater the savings.

With small single-phase systems, these losses have relatively low consequence. But with larger systems, and redundant systems, the cost can really add up.

The average cost of electricity per kW in the US in 2020 was 13.19 cents per kilowatt hour. Using our example results in a cost of about 30 dollars per day, more than ten thousand dollars a year, for the UPS losses only.

If you can improve the efficiency to ninety-five percent you save approximately $5,500 per year.

The larger the system and the more units you have, the higher the cost of losses.

Power Factor

Power factor (PF) is a fundamental concept that must be understood when working with AC power. It is one of the most misunderstood principles in the UPS world by technicians, salesmen, electricians, and end users alike. Often it is confused with the UPS system's efficiency, which is completely different and discussed in the previous Efficiency section.

Basically, power factor is the ratio between real power and apparent power, and is stated as a number between zero and one, one being ideal. Electrical components in the system, such as capacitors and inductors, cause voltage and current to be out of phase, resulting in the real and apparent power being out of phase.

When the power factor is less than one, additional current is needed to complete the same amount of work. The higher the current, the larger the electrical infrastructure is needed, thus increasing cost. We often use the power triangle to visualize power factor. (See Figure 31.)

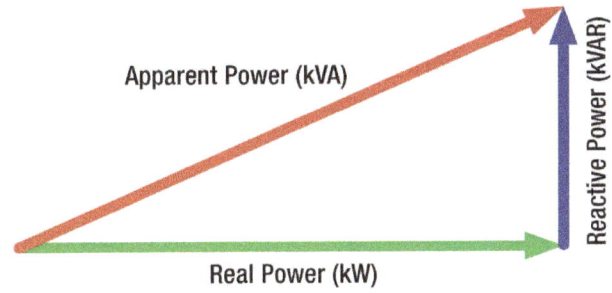

Figure 31

An appropriate explanation used by many instructors to help understand the power triangle is a glass of beer. (See Figure 32.) The glass of beer is the apparent power, everything you pay for. The beer is the real power, the part you drink, and the head or foam is the reactive power, the byproduct of pouring beer into a glass. Because you pay for the whole glass, you want as much beer and as little foam as possible.

Figure32

Now that we know what power factor is, we need to understand the difference between the PF rating of the UPS system and the PF of the load. This can be a difficult concept to understand. Both beginner and veteran technicians often confuse the two.

The rating of the UPS system is what the UPS system can handle without being overloaded. There are watts and volt-amps maximums the inverter can support. The rating of the UPS output power is not the true power factor of the load, it is only what the UPS can support.

So what is the difference between the UPS system's power factor rating and the load's actual power factor? If we look at a simple example of rating vs. actual, it might help clear up the confusion.

Let's think about a typical household circuit and space heater. The household circuit is rated to support roughly 12.5 amps. A typical space heater uses about 12.5 amps when using all its power, the full rating of the circuit. However, if you turn the heater down to half power, the heater will only use about six amps. The circuit is still rated for 12.5 amps, but the load is six amps.

When thinking about the rating of the UPS system vs. the load's power factor, we can think in similar terms. A 100 kVA/80KW UPS system is rated at 0.8 power factor. It can handle a load of 100kVA or 80kW maximum, just as our 12.5 amp circuit can handle a maximum load of 12.5 amps. The UPS system has two limitations, kW and kVA.

The load on the UPS system may be 90kVA and 72kW, making the load's power factor 0.8. But modern loads have power factors closer to one. If the load on the UPS system is 90kVA at a one power factor, the load would also be 90kW, over the 80kW, causing the UPS to be overloaded.

There are two important reasons to understand the difference between the power factor rating of the UPS System, and the power factor of the load: ensuring that you don't overload the system, and that you calculate the correct battery backup time.

Batteries only supply power in kW; therefore, we must always find the kW needed to calculate battery backup time. As an example, we have a 100kVA/80kW UPS system load to 50kVA and 50kW (a power factor of one), and we want to calculate the battery backup time. If battery backup time is calculated using the power factor rating of the UPS system, 0.8, we would calculate this time based on 40kW of load (50 X 0.8=40), and not the true power of 50kW, which would have less backup time than expected. As an example, if we use a typical battery for a system this size, 40 kW would give us approximately twenty minutes of battery runtime, but 50kW would only provide fifteen.

This is also a problem when determining the load on a UPS system. Given the same UPS system above, 100kVA rated at 0.8 power factor, if the load is at 70kVA and 1.0 power factor, how much more load can be added to the UPS system before it is overloaded? Using the rating of the UPS to calculate the load in kW, we will think we have 24kW and 30 more kVA of space. But in reality, we only have 10kW more space. The load is 70kVA and 70kW. If we try to add more than 10kVA to the system, it will overload the system.

A question you may be asking yourself is why we have power factor. Let's make it go away and save all this confusion and additional cost for no benefit. Manufacturers of modern power supplies are working to do just that, and UPS manufacturers are working to keep up with them. Many modern three-phase UPS systems have a power factor rating of one, or unity, but many smaller single-phase units are still rated as low as 0.7. These smaller systems are prone to being overloaded because they have less margin of error when adding loads.

Slew Rate

Slew rate is another misunderstood concept by even the most experienced techs. Many of the ones who do understand it have a hard time explaining it to generator techs, engineers, and customers. However, before we can discuss slew rate, we should talk about sync and what it means to UPS systems.

Sync is short for synchronized, and dictionary.com defines it as "to cause to go on, move, operate, work, etc., at the same rate and exactly together." For UPS systems, we are talking about the UPS inverter and bypass voltage. More specifically, we are talking about them reaching their peak voltage and zero crossing at the same time, meaning they are in phase.

The best explanation I have heard is from a colleague who compares the inverter and bypass voltages of the UPS system to cars on an oval racetrack. When the cars are side by side, the two sources are synced, meaning the bypass voltage and inverter voltage are in phase. In our cars example, the cars are side by side. (See Figure 33.)

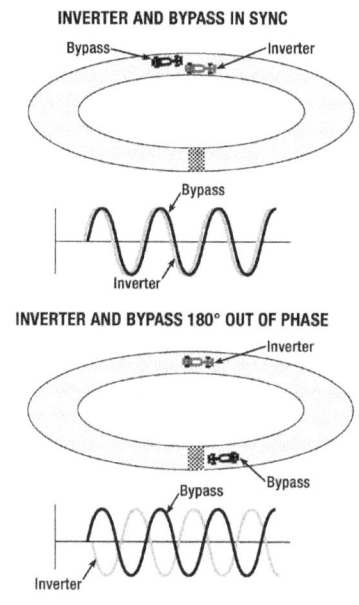

Figure 33

It is important that the voltages are synced and in phase so transfers can occur with no break in power to the critical load. Both the inverter and the bypass line will be 60Hz in North America and 50Hz in other parts of the world, but that does not mean they are in sync; they could be 180 degrees out of phase, or in our analogy, the cars are on opposite sides of the track sync drawing. When they are out of phase, a transfer to bypass cannot happen without a break in power to the load.

Slew rate is how fast the inverter is allowed to speed up or slow down to match itself with the bypass and is measured in Hz/sec. The faster the slew rate, the faster they converge. We cannot change the speed of the bypass; it is set by the utility power company or the onsite generator.

When there is a utility outage, the bypass source will be lost. When it returns, the sources will likely be out of sync, meaning the voltage waveforms are not in phase. You can think of this as if the bypass car made a pit stop. When it returns to the track, the inverter car wants it next to it. Slewing will make this happen.

A slew rate for our inverter race car could be measured in miles/hour. If both cars are traveling at sixty mph, and we allow the inverter car to slew at one mph, the inverter car can change its speed up or down one mph. This means if it wanted to slow down to fifty-eight mph, it would take two hours.

This obviously would not work in reality; it is much too slow. But the principle holds the same if we change to one hundred feet per second, or approximately sixty-eight mph. If we slew at one fps (0.68MPH), we could slow to ninety-five fps (sixty-five MPH) in five seconds. This results in a slow, smooth transition, but it could take a while if the cars are far apart.

On the other hand, if we allow the inverter car to slew at ten fps, it could be down to eighty fps (fifty-five mph) in two seconds and allow the bypass car to catch up much faster. But it would not be as smooth, and the bypass car could overshoot before the inverter car could speed back up to one hundred fps. The trick is to find the happy middle.

Generally, we only see issues with slew rates when generators and UPS systems are not playing well together. The UPS system will continue to alarm that the bypass and inverter voltage are out of phase. Adjusting the slew rate of the UPS system will often correct the issue.

10. UPS Configurations: Single and Parallel

As we have discussed elsewhere, the purpose of a UPS system is to provide uninterruptible power to a critical load. We also know that even the best systems fail.

In addition, some loads are larger than even the largest UPS system can support. To overcome these issues, multiple UPS systems are configured into distinct types of parallel options.

Capacity System

When the critical load is larger than one UPS unit can support, two or more units are connected in parallel to increase capacity. (See Figure 34.)

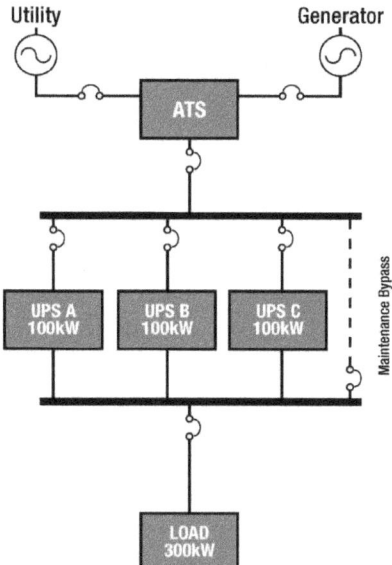

Figure 34

There are not many ways to parallel systems for capacity. Each module will need to feed a common electrical bus that load power can be drawn from. If one module fails, the entire system will transfer to a bypass line, or the load will be lost.

A parallel system used for capacity can be thought of as a single UPS unit, because if any of the modules fail, the system will no longer protect the load.

When discussing or understanding a single UPS system, there is not much to debate. You have a single UPS system, and if it is offline for maintenance, you do not have UPS backup. The same is true if you have a parallel system for capacity. If any units in the system are offline, the critical load does not have UPS backup.

Systems that require multiple units for capacity often include redundancy.

Redundant Systems

All things break and even the most reliable UPS system will fail at some point. Some loads are important enough to need increased reliability. Maybe it's the phone system for a 911 center, or perhaps a loss of operations would cost the company more money than they are willing to risk. These loads often use redundant systems to increase reliability.

A typical engineering definition of redundancy is "the duplication of critical components or functions of a system with the intention of increasing reliability of the system, usually in the case of a backup or fail-safe."

Throughout this book, I've attempted to use IEEE for proper nomenclature to avoid manufacturer bias. However, many of the parallel redundant UPS systems explained in IEEE Standard 446-1995 are either no longer operational or the industry uses a different name. I've used the terms most common in the United States.

A key question to ask when discussing redundant parallel systems is: are there any single points of failure? If so, how many and what is the frequency and method of failure? Is redundancy lost, protective power lost, or does the load drop? And how fast can the system be repaired?

Many systems will have single points of failure. The cost to remove these points is high and introduces complications into the system. The trick is knowing which points are critical and what is the frequency of failure. As with all things, the best system is the one that works for the end user, balancing cost and reliability.

Isolated Redundant

An isolated redundant system is considered N+1 and comprises two units, a primary and a secondary, sometimes called a catcher unit. See the chapter **What is Availability and Why is it Important** to understand the N system.

The primary unit feeds the critical load while the secondary unit feeds the bypass line of the primary unit. If there is a failure of the primary unit, it will transfer to bypass, allowing the secondary unit to continue to protect the load. (See Figure 35.)

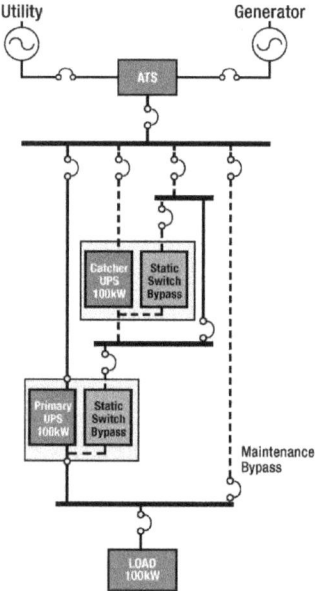

Figure 35

Because the secondary unit is the bypass of the primary unit, a failure would only reduce redundancy. The critical load would still be protected by the primary unit. If there is a failure of the secondary unit while the primary unit is on bypass, the critical load would be unprotected.

There should be an external maintenance bypass that would allow for isolation of the units. This can be one maintenance bypass that isolates both systems simultaneously or two separate ones that would allow each unit to be bypassed. If both maintenance bypasses were operated, the entire system would be in bypass.

An isolated redundant system is a simple system compared to others. It's very versatile in that you do not need to use the same model or manufacturer of UPS systems. When using a two-module system, it's cost effective and requires no complex switch gear. The second system can even be added at a later date.

Disadvantages of an isolated redundant system include single points of failure and complex operation procedures that often lead to mis-operation, resulting in load loss and damage to the UPS systems. If more than one primary UPS unit is needed, the system becomes much more complicated and expensive.

The secondary unit must be able to handle a step load for zero percent to the current load. Most systems today can handle such load increases, but this should be confirmed and even proven before the system is purchased and deployed. There is some doubt in the industry if an isolated redundant system provides more reliability.

Parallel Redundant

A parallel redundant system is also considered N+1. This system uses multiple UPS units in parallel to support the load. If one unit fails, it will automatically be removed from the critical bus and the other units will continue to support the load. (See Figure 36.)

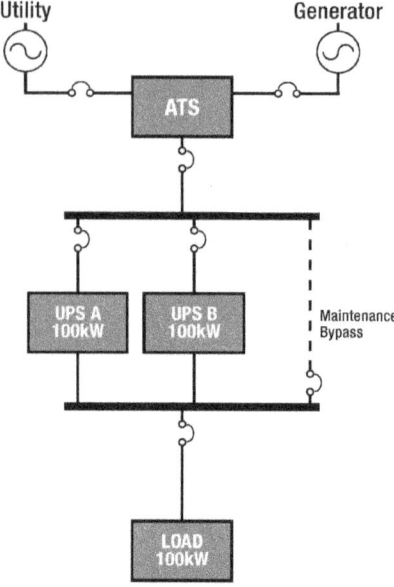

Figure 36

Advantages of the parallel redundant system include:

- There is a lower step load when a module fails. Only the percentage of load carried by the failed system will be loaded to the other modules
- The system can be expanded if built for that option initially
- Operation is simpler than an isolated redundant system

Disadvantages would include:

- All modules must be the same manufacturer, model, and size
- There are still single points of failure
- The load will be unprotected during certain maintenance procedures

Distributed Redundant

In a distributed redundant system, redundancy is located in the distribution system. (See Figure 37.) These systems are complicated and expensive.

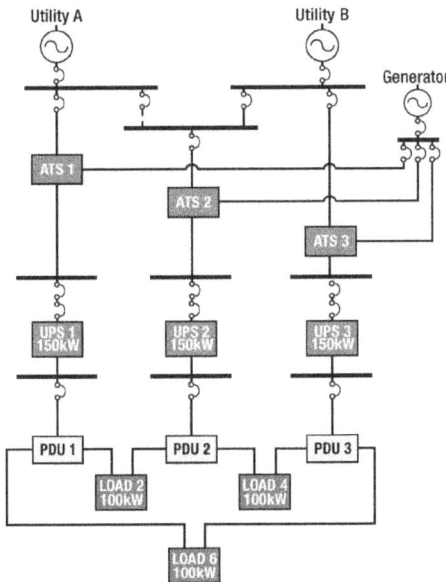

Figure 37

Advantages of a distributed redundant design are:

- Can allow for concurrent maintenance, meaning the load would always be protected by UPS power
- Cost savings over a 2N system
- Two separate power paths for dual- corded equipment, or equipment using point-of-use or rack-mounted static switches.

Disadvantages of the distributed redundant design include:

- High cost because of the extra electrical switch gear, often as much as twice or more of the parts count
- There can still be single points of failure

- UPS systems are not fully loaded increasing inefficiencies. With today's technologies, efficiencies are increasing at low loads, thus reducing this disadvantage

System Plus System

The system plus system design is the most reliable and costly system. These systems can be as complex or as simple as the engineer and end user desires in a efforts to remove every single point failure.

These systems are used to provide the most reliable and available power, and are only used by very large data centers.

The one presented in Figure 38 is one of the simpler designs. It is important to remember other redundant generators, air conditioning, and distribution must be employed to achieve the highest availability, and to reap the benefits of the costly install.

As with all redundant systems, it's advisable to meet with a consultant to discuss the best system for you and your budget.

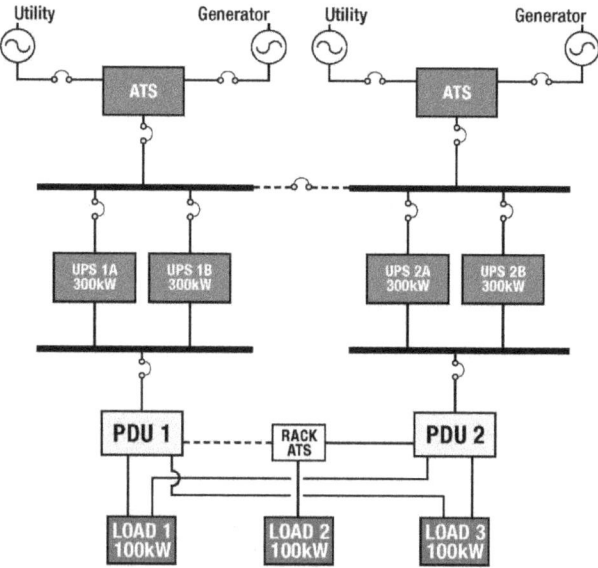

Figure 38

Choosing the Right System

Only the stakeholders can answer which UPS system configuration is right for their application. Seeking guidance from experienced industry professionals is important, but only you know how much risk you can afford.

It's vital that all decision makers know the limits of their system. If building from scratch, this is usually discussed in detail with the design engineer. But when moving into an existing space with existing systems, this can easily be overlooked. Long-term costs need to be factored in when upfront costs are often the deciding factor.

Sometimes the needs of the critical load change. When the system was originally designed and built, a simple UPS system may have been all that was required. But perhaps the company grew and their requirements for a redundant system became necessary. However, no one recognized this. When a major repair is required, these limitations often come to light. When management learns an outage is needed to complete repairs, it is often said it's not possible.

But as the cost of repairing the system without an outage becomes apparent, they realize it can be done, it is just complicated and painful. When discussing the cost of upgrading their UPS system to N+1, or 2N, or their entire data center to Tier 2 or Tier 3, they realize sometimes an outage can be accomplished at a much lower cost.

An important factor that could influence poor decision-making when purchasing a UPS system is not understanding what is being purchased. With the new modular type systems, a salesman can confuse a buyer with terms like internal redundancy or N+1 single unit. They are not lying to the customer, but either the customer doesn't know what they are buying, or the salesman does not know what they are selling. Without a complicated parallel redundant system, there are always single points of failure. Again, the customer must decide if those single points of failure are worth the risks. A cost-benefit analysis must be completed, and all decisionmakers need to be aware of the limitations.

The most important question to ask is, what will downtime cost me? When answering this question, one needs to be brutally honest. Do we need to spend the money for a redundant system, or can we plan our operations to include planned downtime?

Wrong System – Case Study

A longtime customer of ours moved into a new building and kept the same UPS system as the previous user. The original system worked well for that user, someone who needed UPS power, but needed it inexpensively. They could afford scheduled downtime, and worst case would recover if the system failed during a time of production. The system adequately met their needs and budget.

Our customer had different needs, and when they moved into the space, the current system did not meet those needs. But management did not know this, and the original system remained in place supporting their load.

During routine maintenance, the system was transferred to bypass. The inspection revealed a broken control wire that would need to be repaired. This control wire was connected directly to the input transformer and had 480V on it as long as input was applied. Because there was no external maintenance bypass so all power to the unit would need to be removed, which would remove power to the critical load.

As talks progressed with the customer, it became obvious they did not understand the limits of their system. We explained they would need to shut down to complete the repair. As you might imagine, they found this to be unacceptable, even explaining to me that management said the mandate was to repair the system without shutting down the load. They stated this as if because management demanded it, it could be done, ignoring the laws of physics. Several times over the course of the week, I explained that their load would lose power, it was just a matter of time, as the UPS system was in bypass. They could choose the time and circumstances or nature would.

After many meetings and discussions, everyone got on the same page and we completed the repair at a time that had the least negative impact to operations.

Had management understood the limits of their system when they moved into the space, they could have taken steps early in the process to ensure they had the availability they needed. In this case, they didn't need a redundant system, just one with an external maintenance bypass.

11. Modular UPS systems

In the 1990s, American Power Conversion (APC) introduced the Symmetra Power Array. The Symmetra Power Array was a single-phase modular unit ranging in sizes from 4 to16kVA. The modular design allowed for internal redundancy, scalability, and faster serviceability. APC released a three-phase version of the Symmetra called the PX in 2002. This latest UPS system brought revolutionary changes to the industry.

What is Modular

So what is modular and why is it important to a UPS system?

Dictionary.com defines modular as "something built or organized in self-contained units or sections" or "a self-contained unit or item that can be combined or interchanged with others."

We will define a modular UPS system as one that uses smaller self-contained units combined to form a larger functional UPS system. These modules allow for redundancy, expansion and rapid repairs.

The power module is a combination of a rectifier and inverter, two of the major parts of a UPS system. Some manufacturers include a static switch in each power module, where others use a single static switch. The UPS system can consist of two intelligence modules—the main logic of the system—allowing for continued operation if one were to fail.

Advantages of Modular

- N+1 and Time to Repair

    As stated above, each power module consists of a rectifier and inverter, two critical parts of a UPS system. These modules come in specific sizes. A selling point of the modular system is internal redundancy. The system could be set up as N+1 by installing one power module over the total needed for operation.

An example would be if each power module is 10kVA, and the critical load was 25kVA, installing three power modules would support the load. However, if one module failed, the system would transfer to bypass because two 10kVA power modules could not support 25kVA of load. But if you installed a fourth, you would have a redundant power module. Now if one failed, the UPS system would stay online protecting the load while a replacement could be ordered and time scheduled to repair.

Perhaps the most practical advantage of a modular system is the reduced meantime to repair. With the modular system, the UPS system can be repaired within minutes of the parts arriving on site. You simply remove the failed module and insert the new operational one. A screwdriver is all that is required.

A traditional UPS system requires the parts be removed by disconnecting the power and control wires. Also, the failed component will need to be unbolted from the actual unit frame and the reverse to install the replacement parts. After the parts are installed, a full test will need to be conducted, often taking hours.

- Scalability

Another selling point is the pay-as-you-grow concept, or scalability. During the original construction, you install the electrical infrastructure for the larger UPS system but you only buy the number of power modules you need now. If in the future you need more UPS power, you buy additional power modules and install them. There is no costly downtime or expense to complete the electrical upgrade.

You can only expand the UPS system to its maximum capacity, so be sure when you make the original purchase you buy the maximum frame size you forecast to meet your needs.

- Hot Swappable

One of the original selling points of the modular system was the hot-swappable power modules. If one of these modules failed, it could be removed and replaced while the system stayed online protecting the critical load. It was even suggested that the customer could replace the failed parts, reducing the overall cost.

But as the understanding of arc flash dangers have increased, NFPA 70E, Standard for Electrical Safety in the Workplace, and the National Electric Code no longer allow most of the components to be hot-swapped.

Limits of Modular Systems

Redundancy has become a very important factor in UPS systems, as the requirement for uptime has increased. Manufacturers have done an outstanding job of selling modular UPS systems as redundant. But what redundancy does a modular UPS system actually bring?

If we look at a modular UPS system, such as the APC ISX systems by Schneider Electric, we get a better understanding of this redundancy. If a power module fails and the system is configured correctly, the UPS will stay online and the critical load remains protected by UPS power.

With the modular battery systems, a failed battery will not compromise the entire system, as there are many parallel strings. This is discussed in more details in the section on **Modular Batteries**.

These advantages, combined with the reduced time to repair, have greatly increased the time the critical load is protected. But we need to be careful that we understand the limits of this redundancy. There are still single points of failure in these systems.

As noted earlier, the static switch is a module, but often there is only one in the UPS unit, not one in each power module. (See Figure 39.) If the static switch fails, there is no way to get the critical load to bypass to allow for repairs. Sometimes when a static switch fails, the load will be lost immediately.

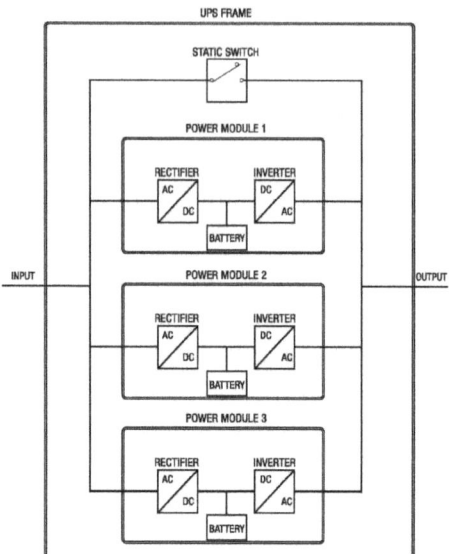

Figure 39

Certain manufacturers have solved this issue by including a static switch in each module. (See Figure 40.) As always, it's important that a complete understanding of the limitations of the system are understood before purchasing. What are the single points of failure and what is the impact when that point fails?

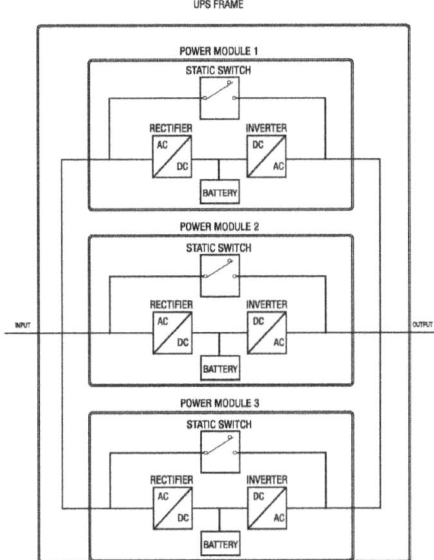

Figure 40

Cost

The upfront or capital cost of a modular UPS system can be more than two times a traditional UPS system. Additionally, maintenance contracts can be considerably higher than a traditional UPS system, which means the total cost of ownership can be a major disadvantage to a modular UPS system.

But even this cost could be lower than the cost of two or more traditional UPS units.

Types of Modular Systems

In the 1990s, APC introduced the first modular UPS system known as the Matrix. The small single-phase system was constructed of two modules; one contained the rectifier, inverter, and static switch, while the other included the input and output landing blocks for the power cables. If the rectifier or inverter failed, the module could be replaced with only a screwdriver.

However, it did not have the advantages of many modular UPS systems, the ability to scale or possess internal redundancy.

Some systems sold today as modular resemble the APC Matrix, only on a larger scale. Parts of the system are built as a unit and can be identified as failed and replaced more quickly than traditional components.

There are several types of modular UPS systems. It is critical that when comparing different modular systems, you understand the details. What makes it modular? What needs to be done to replace a module? How do I expand it to a larger system? Can I shrink it if my load decreases?

Not all modular UPS systems are equal. Care must be taken by the buyer and specifying engineer to be sure they understand what they are buying.

UPS Sizing vs. Battery Backup

A common misunderstanding of a modular system is what adding power modules and batteries will do. In several of these systems, the inverter and rectifier are contained in modules. Each module is a certain size depending on the type of system. Adding a power module will increase the capacity of the UPS system. The APC ISX 100, a 100kW system, uses up to ten 10kW modules. For each module added to the system, you increase its capacity by 10kW.

This differs from batteries, which are also built-in modules. Increasing battery modules increases the backup time, not UPS system capacity.

As an example, a customer purchases a 50kW modular UPS system with fifteen minutes of battery backup time. The system will be installed with five 10kW power modules and eight battery module strings. The following year, the customer's load is increasing and they want to upsize their UPS system to an 80kW. They simply purchase three more power modules and have them installed. This requires no downtime or upgrade in the electrical infrastructure, which would have been built for the 100kW system. However, if battery modules are not increased with the increase in power modules, the battery run time will decrease.

On the other side of the coin: the customer has a 50kW solution with five battery modules and fifteen minutes of battery backup, but they want to increase the battery runtime to twenty-five minutes. Purchasing several more battery modules will increase the battery runtime, but it will not increase the total capacity of the UPS system; it would still be a 50kW UPS.

Power and battery modules are only related in that if you increase power modules and add more load to your system, you will decrease battery backup time. Conversely, if you add battery modules you will increase backup time but not the load capacity of the UPS system.

This is a critical concept that I often see misunderstood but one that is key to understanding the basic principles of growing your UPS system to meet your increasing power needs.

12. How to Achieve Availability

While writing this book, I went back and forth on whether to include this section. I felt it was important for readers to understand the difference, but then I would think these concepts are for decisionmakers of larger data centers, and they would pay consultants to explain them. Ultimately, I included it because I feel it's important for everyone to understand the concepts at a basic level.

When there is a problem with your UPS system—and there will be a problem—some of these concepts may be discussed in the ensuing conversations. Sometimes industry jargon will be used by someone who may not completely understand it. I hope to introduce these concepts so when they are discussed, follow-up questions can be explored to provide the best solution.

Availability vs. Reliability

All things break. That's reality. Even the best UPS systems sometimes fail; its's only a matter of time. The question is, do you want to be in control of when it happens, or just let it occur whenever?

When the failure occurs, depending on its severity, someone will mention the tier systems, redundancy, single points of failure, concurrent maintenance, availability, hardening, and N+1 or 2N+1. Some of these we have discussed elsewhere in greater detail.

Two terms often used interchangeably are availability and reliability, but they are not the same. According to Merriam-Webster, available means "present or ready for immediate use..." Availability is "the quality or state of being available." We can refine the definition of availability in the critical power world as the quality or state of protected power being present and ready for immediate use.

Reliability is defined as "the state of being reliable or the state of which something is dependable."

For engineers, the difference between availability and reliability comes down to what some would consider complicated math. But simply put, availability is the percentage of hours that the critical power will be present and ready to use when compared to the total number of hours measured against. An example could help explain.

There is a total of 8,760 hours in a year. If your single UPS system is taken offline for maintenance twice a year for five hours each time, uninterrupted power will be available for 8,750 of those hours, an availability of 99.886 percent. If we stretch this out to five years using the same ten hours per year for routine maintenance and an additional ten hours to replace batteries, the availability will drop to (43,800-60)/43,800, or 99.86 percent availability.

Reliability, on the other hand, is how much time uninterrupted power is present when you expect it. So if you are planning maintenance, you don't count those hours. Reliability is how long the system is *not* broken.

In the same example above, if our system is offline for an unplanned forty-eight hours because of a system failure, our reliability is (43800-48)/43800, or 99.89 percent. In reality, reliability will always be higher than availability.

The metric used in the critical power industry to measure and therefore influence the decision-making process is availability.

To help keep things simple, we will only discuss availability. If UPS power is not available, we are at risk. We know from earlier that if our critical load loses power for even a fraction of a second, we will lose our operations, sometimes for hours. Therefore, it is wise to plan to lose operations, or better to stop them, when maintenance is planned that will result in the loss of protected power.

Availability and the Five 9s

Our example above is helpful when explaining availability and reliability. But in the industry, it is common to discuss availability using the five 9s. Each 9 is the percentage of availability that a system theoretically has.

As an example, a five 9s system would have 99.999 percent of availability, and a four 9s would have 99.99 percent. This works well when comparing various types of systems, particularly when using the tier systems discussed next.

More importantly, we need to know what our availability is when we design and install our systems. Calculating our availability every three to five years will tell us how well we did but won't help us when we are setting budgets and planning maintenance.

The fallacy of the 9s

We often hear people discuss the need for five 9s but there are problems with this thinking. One is basic math. For a system to be available 99.999 percent of the time, it could only not have protected power for 5.25 minutes per year. Basically, you could do no maintenance.

A more fundamental problem is, does your system need five 9s, or can you survive with three or four 9s? Table 3 below shows how each of the five 9s relate to the unavailability of a system.

Table 3

Number of 9s	Minutes Unavailable/Year
Five (99.999%)	5.26
Four (99.99%)	52.56
Three (99.9%)	525.6

Even the most basic systems can provide three 9s or higher.

We can all probably agree that shutting down a data center for almost nine hours a year is not reasonable. But what about a maintenance window for twelve hours where the load is supported by bypass?

It's also important to note that just because UPS power is not available, it does not mean there is no power to the critical load. You could be operating from utility power or an emergency generator.

Achieving five 9s is exponentially more expensive compared to four 9s and is only financially achievable by the largest companies.

Ideal System on a Budget

What is the perfect system for a client? We have discussed this throughout the book and there is no one-size-fits-all answer. With some outside-the-box thinking, deployment of A/B power supplies, and the use of low-cost point of use static switches, options not generally deployed can add availability and reliability to your system.

One option to save money and still retain a level of redundancy is to use two UPS systems with internal maintenance bypass and integrated distribution. (See Figure 41.) One system would feed A power supplies while the other would feed B power supplies. When maintenance needs to be completed on one system, the other would support the load. The same would be true if one system failed.

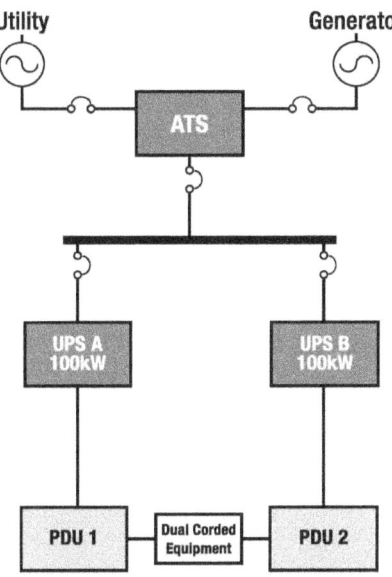

Figure 41

While maintenance or repairs are being performed, there is a loss of redundancy, but without building a tier-three or higher system, there is always a possibility for loss of redundancy.

With creative thinking, a second option is using one UPS system to support A power supplies and utility to support the B power supplies. This would require additional distribution and upfront cost. (See Figure 42.)

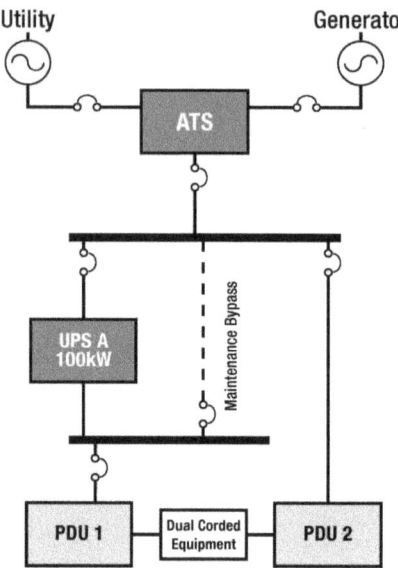

Figure 42

There is also increased risk that if there is a utility power loss and your A power supply fails, a piece of equipment will lose power but the entire data center will not lose power. An additional UPS system could be purchased later to protect the B power supplies with little impact on operations.

With any option employed, all stakeholders must know the pros and cons, and how they will impact long-term operations. It is well worth paying a neutral consultant upfront to help with the decision-making process.

13. Maintenance

A good friend of mine owns rental properties and flips houses. He is one of the hardest working people I know, and he is always in a hurry. Always moving on to the next project or task.

One day he had knee surgery and couldn't drive, but he still wanted to get some work done. He asked me to meet him at his house and chauffeur him around in his truck. As we were driving, I noticed the oil light would come on and the pressure would drop.

"It happens when you make left turns," he told me. "I need to take it in for repairs." When I asked if he checked the oil lately, he smiled and laughed. We stopped at the next gas station and I pulled the dipstick. There was no oil on it. We added several quarts and the light did not return.

My friend is not a huge fan of preventive maintenance. He doesn't take the time needed to complete it up front. The problem is when we don't do proper maintenance, equipment fails prematurely and at the worst possible moment. His truck breaking down would have been very painful for him. He would lose a day of work and it would cost money to get it fixed.

If a UPS system fails, it could be much more costly. Often companies lose thousands of dollars for every minute their load is down. It's difficult to know the exact cost of data center downtime, but a study by the Ponemon Institute noted the average cost is fifty-six hundred dollars a minute, and almost thirty percent of that downtime was from UPS system failures.

Preventive Maintenance

If preventive maintenance is the best way to prevent failures in our UPS systems, the next question is, what maintenance is needed? We will discuss common practices in the industry but each manufacturer has recommendations that should be reviewed and followed.

Some modern systems run self-tests when started and at pre-program intervals. If a problem is found, an alert will be generated and corrective action taken.

It is recommended that UPS systems undergo a complete preventive maintenance procedure a minimum of once a year. During the visit, the following should be performed, and a detailed report supplied by the service company.

- Record input and output power parameters and compare with front panel
- Review operation with site personnel
- Clean unit
- Visual inspection for swollen capacitors or signs of heat
- Review alarm logs
- Run self-test if applicable
- Check protection settings if applicable
- Check power supplies if applicable
- Check operation of fans
- Check input and output voltage and current waveforms
- Monitor operation of UPS system operation on generator if applicable
- Transfer to bypass
- Replace air filters
- Perform any firmware upgrades provided by the manufacturer

UPS System Failure

UPS systems are quite complex and require very specialized training and tools to troubleshoot and repair. The most important thing a user can do is to understand how to operate their UPS system and its maintenance bypass, if equipped.

When a failure occurs—and one will occur—individuals often forget the training they underwent five years prior when the unit was installed and started. Sometimes the people who were there for the training have moved on. Making sure that written procedures are available, including the service provider's name and phone number, as well as the model and serial number of the UPS system, can be invaluable when a failure occurs. It's also a good idea to review operation of your equipment whenever maintenance is completed. This helps ensure that responsible parties are familiar with operating the unit in an emergency.

Failure to Follow Recommendations—A Case Study

A customer we had supported for many years was planning to upgrade their UPS system the next fiscal year. However, the batteries in their current system were at the end of their life. We recommended they replace them, but they declined, hoping to save money.

A few weeks later the UPS system went into alarm with weak batteries. We dispatched a technician to check the system and found several bad jars. We sent a proposal to the customer, and the bad batteries were replaced.

A couple of months after this, the customer called telling us they had a power outage and the UPS system was unable to support the load. We sent out another technician and found more failed batteries. The customer again wanted to replace only the bad jars; they were planning to replace the UPS system in only three months.

As we reviewed all the data and the history of the plant, we did not feel it would survive the three months and recommended they replace the batteries immediately. We also had safety concerns; we did not feel comfortable returning the current batteries to operation.

After speaking with our sales team, I had a rough estimate of what it would cost to replace the plant–fifteen thousand dollars. The customer was concerned about spending this money for only a few months of use. I asked a question during the discussions and explained only they could answer it. If the power failed immediately and the load were to drop again, would it cost more than fifteen thousand dollars? Everyone in the room nodded, and the CFO and CIO stated it would cost far more. The decision was simple; they needed to replace the batteries ASAP.

Not all decisions are this easy and straightforward, and often procuring the funds is a long and difficult process. When this is the case, it is even more important that a good preventive maintenance program is in effect and budgeting for replacement is made before there is a failure.

14. When to Hire a Consultant

There is a saying in life, "Proper Planning Prevents Poor Performance." A variation is, "Failing to plan is planning to fail." Many times, the planning is simple and you don't even realize you are doing it. For instance, checking the weather before leaving the house, or watching the morning news for a traffic report so you are not late for work. Most of us have made the mistake of not preparing for the weather, and we are cold or wet for a day. Or we've gotten stuck in traffic we could have avoided had we spent a few more minutes preparing.

These are relativity inexpensive events, things that can easily be corrected, or the pain is temporary. But buying a UPS system is a decision that will last many years. With a system and installation that meets your needs now and in the foreseeable future, you can save a great deal of money, time, and heartache. But the opposite is also true; poor planning will cause years of extra expense and frustration, as a key element of your critical power infrastructure does not meet your needs.

Types of Consulting Services

MEP Firms

When building a new, large data center, a design firm known as an MEP (mechanical, electrical, and plumbing) is often used. These include a mechanical and electrical engineer. Some MEPs will have an architect on staff, and other times they will collaborate with a different company.

These engineers are responsible for the entire building design. This includes lights, life, safety, power for air conditioning equipment, bathrooms, etc. They often rely on manufacturer representatives to keep them apprised of the latest equipment designs; without them it would be impossible for an engineer to know everything about every product on the market.

Manufacturers court MEP firms regularly. This is not to say that MEP firms are unethical or biased. The company they recommend could be the best fit or may be the easiest or most responsive to work with. But it is important to ask more probing questions when a firm recommends a certain product.

Questions such as why should we choose this manufacturer over another one? What are the advantages of this model over another model? What is the total cost of ownership of the recommended manufacturer over an another?

There are MEP firms that specialize in data centers. When building a new data center, it would be a good idea to talk to several of these companies. What experience do they have? What type of products have they worked with in the past? And does their experience match your needs?

MEP firms frequently work for the end user and are a great resource. Their main responsibilities are to ensure the finished product is safe and meets their client's needs. When designing and building from the ground up, an MEP will probably be needed.

The Manufacturer

My son was approaching the age when a cell phone was in his near future. We were all excited about how it would improve our lives; because his mother and I split time with him, a phone would give all of us more communication.

About this time, the PTA emailed us advising that the attorney general was presenting a seminar at the local high school on internet safety. My wife and I decided to attend, hoping to glean some useful information to help protect our son.

The presentation scared me with how easy it is to get information about someone. My wife and I both learned a tremendous amount, but one major takeaway was something that most of us know but can rarely put into words.

There is no such thing as a free lunch. You are either buying or selling. When something is free, such as social media, then you, or your information, is the product being bought or sold.

Everyone should keep this in mind when buying products and services. Using a manufacturer as a consultant often comes at no charge. Depending on the size of the system you plan to purchase, the sales reps and applications engineers will spend a lot of resources helping in the design processes. Much of this information is helpful, and normally honest. Most in the profession are ethical. But it is key to remember that they will push solutions that work best with their product and post-sales services.

When relying on a manufacturer to assist with the design of your data center, it would be a good idea to consult several manufacturers. Compare not only the initial price of the equipment but also the long-term maintenance cost. Most importantly, are you getting what you need now and in the future?

Third-Party Service Companies

Third-party service companies are a great resource for consultation. They provide no-charge services and are often vendor agnostic. They can offer a solution that best fits your unique needs.

Like any vendor, a third-party service provider should be fully vetted. You want to know how much experience they have and how long they've been in business. What products do they sell and service? It would also be a good idea to have them provide references of their previous work.

An advantage of a third-party company is they may have contracts with several manufacturers. This allows them to make recommendations that best fit the end user's needs. But again, the key to making the best decision is to ask and understand why they recommend a specific model over another.

Which Is Right for Me?

My wife and I decided to build a house on our family farm. I was discussing this at lunch with my longtime boss. We discussed the fee for an architect for a few minutes, and then he said something profound, or rather, one of those things we know but often forget. The final product always starts with a good design. I would do well to spend more money upfront to be sure I get everything I want.

If I were redoing my basement or upgrading a bathroom or kitchen, I would use a reputable contractor and work with them and save the money on an architect. The same would hold true if I were installing a small UPS system or replacing one that was working fine but was at the end of its service life. I would use my UPS service company, my trusted electrician, or the local UPS sales representative.

But if I were putting in an addition or building a house from the ground up, I would use an architect. I would want someone who knows the ins and outs of building a home, or how to use space, and long-term savings in energy. Armed with this information, I would contact a builder and tradesperson to complete the tasks.

The same should be used when building a new data center or upgrading an existing one. Often MEP firms will have people on staff who specialize in data center designs. These can be hired to look after your interests.

There is no right or wrong answer to when to use a consultant and which consultant service to hire. Each has its advantages and disadvantages, and each will serve a different need. But it's important to know who they are ultimately working for—you, themselves, or someone else.

PART II
BATTERIES

15. Introduction

For a UPS system to function when the input power fails, a stored energy device is needed. Until recently, lead-acid batteries were the most common type of stored energy. As of this writing, lead-acid batteries are still the predominant technology used in UPS applications. With the increased use of batteries for electric vehicles and off-grid solar systems, the cost of lithium-ion batteries is decreasing. As the price decreases, they will be used more often, and the cheaper they will become. But the process will take time, and in the interim lead-acid batteries will remain the prevalent technology.

How a Battery Works

An in-depth understanding of how lead-acid batteries work is not needed, but a basic one can be helpful.

At the basic level, electrical power requires a difference in electrons, known as potential, between two points. When a load such as a light bulb is connected between these points, current will flow from one point of potential, through the light bulb, to the other point, causing the bulb to light. A lead-acid battery is a chemical device with one post more positive than the other. (See Figure 42.)

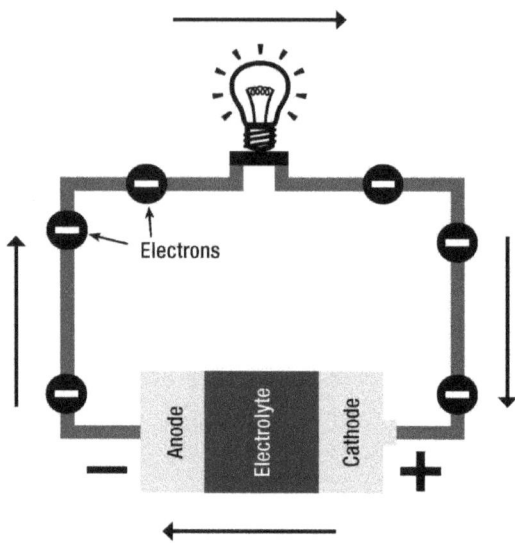

Flow of electrons around the curcuit

Figure 42

The fundamental job of a battery is to convert potential chemical energy into electrical energy. For us, this electrical energy is used to support the UPS inverter. The basic parts of a lead-acid cell are:

- Positive Plate – Lead Alloy
- Negative Plate – Pure Lead
- Electrolyte – Sulfuric Acid

When a battery is fully charged, the negative plate is pure lead, the positive plate is lead dioxide, and the electrolyte is a mixture of sulfuric acid and water.

When a load is connected, electrons travel from the negative plate, through the load device, and to the positive plate. The electrolyte transfers electrons to the negative plate. During the discharge process, the plates and electrolyte change chemically as they work. (See Figure 43.)

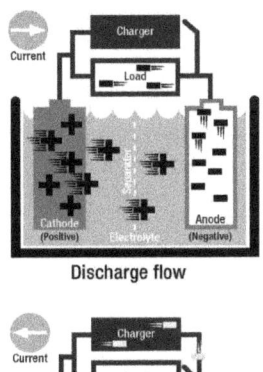

Discharge flow

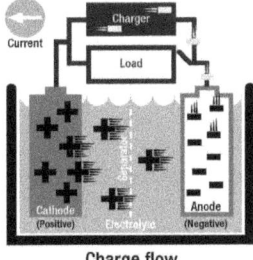

Charge flow

Figure 43

When the electrolyte is depleted, has no more electrons to give up, the battery is discharged, the electrolyte is mostly water and the plates will be lead sulfate.

When power is applied to the battery, a recharge cycle will begin. The charger forces current through the battery, causing a chemical change opposite of the discharge. When fully charged the negative plate will again be pure lead, the positive plate lead dioxide, and the electrolyte sulfuric acid. (See Figure 43.)

16. Types of Lead-Acid Batteries

Vented

There are two basic categories of lead-acid batteries used with UPS systems: vented and valve regulated lead acid. (VRLA).

Vented batteries are filled with liquid electrolyte and have transparent cases. (See Figure 44.) Because of the liquid electrolyte, they are often referred to as flooded batteries or wet cells.

Figure 44

Vented lead-acid batteries have a useful life two to three times that of VRLA batteries when maintained correctly. In addition, if proper maintenance is completed, failing batteries can be identified early and corrective action taken. This reduces the risk of a sudden UPS system failure because of a bad battery.

There are several disadvantages to vented batteries. These disadvantages have caused most users to switch to VRLA batteries. Vented batteries are much more expensive to install and maintain. They also require a much larger footprint.

Because the electrolyte is in liquid form, some jurisdictions requires a system to capture the electrolyte should a container break and the fluid leak out. This adds additional expense.

When batteries are overcharged, explosive hydrogen gas can be produced. Some jurisdictions also require a system to monitor for hydrogen gas and exhaust it if the level exceeds one to two percent.

Value Regulated Lead-Acid

Value regulated lead-acid batteries, VRLA, come in two varieties, absorbent glass matt, AGM, and gel. AGMs are built by saturating a fiberglass mat in the electrolyte, where gels use a putty-like substance. (See Figure 45.)

Figure 45

The major advantages of VRLA batteries are space-saving and lower maintenance costs. Two major disadvantages of VRLA batteries are their short life compared to vented batteries, and the inability to see inside them. Because we can't see what is going on inside, they sometimes need to be replaced early to ensure system reliability.

17. Choosing the Right Battery System

Sizing Batteries

Choosing the correct battery for your application is not as simple as determining the backup time required. There are distinct types of lead-acid batteries as discussed in the section **Types of Lead-Acid Batteries**. However, how much backup time you need is the first question. This answer will help decide what battery type you should consider.

In the past, larger UPS systems approximately 500kVA and up, would use vented batteries, but recently we have seen many with multiple strings of VRLAs. Once you know the backup time needed, you will want to determine if multiple strings are an option. There are advantages and disadvantages to each as discussed in **Redundant Strings**.

The vendor supplying the UPS—or the engineer doing the design—can help with these decisions.

Backup Time

One of the most common questions technicians get is, "How much backup time do I have?" Most of today's UPS systems can tell you this from the front panel or a web interface. Some, however, won't display this information until the system is running on batteries. That is not very helpful when deciding before an outage occurs.

Another key factor to the system displaying the correct backup time is if the battery information programmed into the UPS system is correct. If the information entered is incorrect, the backup time displayed will be incorrect. As the saying goes, *garbage in, garbage out.*

A more reliable option is to have the backup time calculated by the company doing your battery or UPS system maintenance. Battery manufacturers supply run-time charts that can be used by knowledgeable persons to calculate the run time given in your specific situation.

If knowing your backup time is critical for operations, having someone calculate the backup time and compare that with the information supplied by the UPS system is the best practice.

Redundant Strings

Several things can increase reliability besides performing routine maintenance. Options include using multiple strings, installing a monitoring system, or using a modular battery topology. The options discussed here, while useful, are not a substitute for a solid preventive maintenance program, including replacing batteries at end of life.

The major disadvantage of a single string of batteries is the multiple single points of failure. Think of a battery string as a chain, with each cell being a link. Many modern UPS systems require 240 cells in series to make a battery string. In our analogy, that would be 240 links. If one cell fails, the entire string fails, just as if one link breaks in the chain, the entire chain is useless. (See Figure 46.) If multiple strings, or chains, are used when a cell or link fails, the others will continue to operate.

Figure 46

Multiple strings of batteries require a larger initial investment and maintenance cost, including replacement at end of life. They also have a greater footprint, reducing space for IT equipment.

It is impractical and unnecessary to use multiple strings of vented batteries. It would be cost-prohibitive, and if redundancy at that level is required, choosing a parallel UPS configuration is a better option.

Modular Batteries

An alternative option growing in popularity over the past decade is modular batteries. Modular batteries are configured with small battery jars inside a larger container. (See Figure 47.) Several of these containers or modules make a string. Because the jars are smaller, multiple modules are paralleled in a cabinet, increasing redundancy, often in the same size footprint as a single string of traditional VRLA batteries.

Figure 47

Modular batteries possess additional advantages over traditional battery solutions. The UPS systems contain a built-in monitor that records applicable data during a pre-scheduled self-test or discharge. When the system finds a weak module, it will generate alerts, allowing the suspected module to be identified and replaced.

Modular batteries can be replaced relativity quickly as compared to a traditional VRLA plant. For example, a UPS system loaded to 80kW with ten minutes of battery backup could have its batteries replaced by one person in as little as two hours. Additionally, the system could stay online, allowing the critical load to be protected by the UPS system during the replacement.

A more traditional VRLA plant would require two people and two hours. The system would need to be bypassed, placing the critical load at risk.

There are two major disadvantages to modular battery design. They are typically 1.5 times the cost of traditional battery solutions. Also, you must stay with the original manufacturer, eliminating competitive bidding.

18. Battery Maintenance

The number one preventable UPS system failure is batteries. With proper maintenance, a battery failure resulting in loss of power to the critical load is preventable. A basic maintenance plan is outlined below, but your needs and type of battery will determine what program you need.

A basic vented battery preventive maintenance—or PM—program should be completed quarterly.

Three times a year the following should be completed:

- Collecting and recording one hundred percent of all cell voltages
- Collecting and recording ten percent of all cell-specific gravities
- Checking all cell electrolyte levels and adding distilled water as needed
- Performing a visual inspection for sulfation (small sulfate crystals form on the plates from being undercharged, reducing the battery's capacity), cracked plates, excessive sediment, and general health.

Once annually everything completed on the quarterly plus the following should be done:

- Collecting and recording one hundred percent of cell resistances
- Collecting and recording one hundred percent of specific gravities
- Collecting and recording one hundred percent of all cell inter-cell resistances
- Cleaning all jars as needed
- One hundred percent re-torques if inter-cell resistances indicate connection issues.

Valve regulated batteries, sometimes called maintenance-free, still require maintenance, although substantially less. The following should be completed twice a year:

- Collect and record one hundred percent of jar voltages
- Collect and record one hundred percent inter-cell link resistances
- Re-torque all hardware yearly

All data collected should be recorded, stored, and reviewed for changes over the baselines or previous PMs.

A final comment about battery maintenance: we often see customers who have maintenance programs in place. Annual or semiannual battery PMs are completed, the results reviewed, and recommendations forwarded to the customer. Often those recommendations involve the need to replace an aging battery plant soon.

However, the customer may forget or get too busy to replace the battery plant. Within months of our recommendation, the customer may call us and explain that the UPS system is in alarm and their load is off. Murphy's law states this will happen late at night, on a weekend, or during a holiday, the worst possible times.

When we arrive at the site, we find there was a utility outage and the batteries have failed. Depending on the type of battery and time of day, we may not be able to acquire a replacement plant for days, and sometimes weeks. This leaves the customer's load unprotected until the batteries can be procured and replaced.

Proactive replacement of batteries is one of the easiest and best things that can be done to ensure a UPS system can do its job, which is to protect the critical load.

Battery Monitors

Many new UPS systems have built-in battery testing programs. The system will run a test routinely and alert the user if there is a suspected problem. However, the UPS system can only test the batteries as a string, it cannot identify if a single cell or jar is weak.

There are also external battery monitoring systems that keep tabs on how the battery plant is performing. Many of these systems will allow for monitoring of individual cells. When an external battery monitoring system is used, it is most economical to install it during the initial installation or when batteries are replaced. It is also critical that someone in the organization knows how to use the system and trusts it.

Battery Life

Batteries have a finite life, much like car tires. Even when proper maintenance is performed, they wear out and need to be replaced. It's common to hear in the UPS industry that a ten-year VRLA battery only lasts five years. This has held throughout my career with a few exceptions. Vented batteries have a longer useful life than VRLAs, but seldom do they make it to their published twenty-year life.

Several factors affect the life of a battery, including temperature, depth of discharge, and how often they are discharged. IEEE Standard 1188-2005 "Recommended Practice for Maintenance, Testing, and Replacement of Valve-Regulated Lead-Acid (VRLA) Batteries for Stationary Applications," states that for every fifteen degrees F above seventy-seven degrees, a battery's life will be reduced by half.

- Depth of Discharge – The deeper a battery is discharged, the shorter its life span. UPS systems have circuits in place that will only allow a battery to discharge to a safe level, preventing early failures because of deep discharges.
- Cyclic Life – One of the major determining factors in a battery's life is the number of cycles. A cycle is one discharge followed by a recharge, normally to eighty percent of its capacity. Each battery has a finite number of cycles.
- Recharge Voltage and Rate (specific to VRLA) – Charging at a higher voltage than recommended by the manufacturer, or charging the battery faster, can cause cell dry out. The water absorbed in the glass matt evaporates, and because the battery is sealed, it cannot be replaced. When too much water has been removed, the battery will need to be replaced.

Keeping the battery room cool is one of the best ways to ensure batteries will have the longest life. Choosing the proper size and type of batteries to match the need is a critical step early in the process and will also help extend battery life.

Warranties

Battery warranties are a tricky thing. Each manufacturer writes its own warranty and each can be different. If a warranty is important when deciding which battery to purchase, it should be discussed with someone knowledgeable in the field and who has experience working with battery manufacturer's warranty claims.

With VRLAs, it is highly recommended that when it's time to replace your batteries, you use the company that is completing the maintenance on the batteries. Most manufacturers will replace a battery that has failed in the first year, and some even longer, but they will require detailed information. A reputable service company will have collected and stored this data during PMs. The company will also work with the manufacturer to replace the battery.

Also, the manufacturer will often only cover the battery and not the labor to replace it. A service company may cover the labor as part of its value-added services.

Vented battery warranties can be more confusing. These batteries have what is termed a pro-rata warranty for much longer than the full replacement, as is common with VRLAs. This warranty will provide a credit toward replacing the batteries when it has been proven they have failed during the warranty period.

The trick with this type of warranty is the credit. The manufacturer will calculate how much of the battery value has been used and how much is left. It will credit the remaining value to the purchase of a new battery plant or the failed cells. Depending on the age of the battery, it is sometimes less expensive to purchase a new battery plant without using the warranty.

It is also important to note that when the batteries are replaced under warranty, the original date of sale is the date the warranty begins. As an example, if you purchased batteries in 2010 with a twenty-year warranty and replaced them in 2020 under the warranty, the new battery plant has ten years left on the warranty.

Again, a reputable service company will help you through the process.

19. Long Run Times: A Case Study

Many times throughout my career a customer has asked for several hours of battery backup time. My next question is, "What about air conditioning?" Air conditioning systems are not powered by UPS systems because of the large load they draw when starting up.

All loads powered by a UPS system generate heat. This heat is removed with air conditioning. If there is no power to support the air conditioners, the heat cannot be removed. At some point, the heat will rise to a point where the UPS system will shut down due to high temperature. But until then, the batteries will be subjected to excessive heat and damage.

One Saturday afternoon, I received a call from one of our customers. They had an emergency and needed immediate service. Their equipment was shutting down and just a few minutes before they called me, the UPS system shut down. All critical operations had stopped.

When I arrived onsite, I suspected what had happened. The building and surrounding blocks had lost utility power, the UPS system had run on batteries until the batteries were exhausted, and the system subsequently shut down.

However, as I entered the data center, I felt like I had stepped into a sauna. The customer explained that when they lost power, they operated on battery power for about two hours. At about the two-hour mark, their load equipment started shutting down, and eventually so did the UPS system. He explained they had four hours of battery run time and wanted to know why the system had shut down early.

After power returned, I inspected the UPS system and reviewed the alarm logs. The system shut down due to high temperature. The customer did have over four hours of backup, but had no generator and no air conditioning system. Their servers and UPS system shut down on over-temperature.

The high temperature damaged the batteries, which would need to be replaced. It would take several days for the batteries to arrive, and during that time they would have no battery backup. For some reason the customer was not aware of this pitfall.

When long backup times are required, it is best to use professionals who understand the limits of the UPS system and can suggest a way to remove heat. The preferred solution would be the installation of an emergency generator, which is designed to support UPS and air conditioning systems. The monies for the high initial cost, maintenance, and replacement of a large battery plant could be used to purchase a generator.

20. Summary of Other Technologies

There are technologies other than lead-acid batteries that can store energy. That energy can then be transformed by the inverter to support the critical load. As a majority of UPS systems are supported by lead-acid batteries, most of this book and our discussions have centered on them. But for completeness' sake, other systems are briefly discussed here. This list is not exhaustive and only an introduction to the current technologies being explored.

Flywheels

Flywheels have been around for decades and have been used with varying degrees of success in the UPS industry. A flywheel stores kinetic energy in a wheel that spins between eight thousand and fifty thousand RPM. When there is a power outage, the momentum in the flywheel drives a generator, producing DC voltage to support the inverter.

Flywheels will only support a load for several seconds and are used when the generator bus is extremely reliable, such as in hospitals. How long a flywheel will provide backup power depends on its size and how much load it is supporting. Sometimes they are used in combination with batteries. The flywheel provides a brief ride-through during most short outages, and the batteries are used for longer outages.

Lithium-Ion Batteries

Lithium-ion batteries are an electrochemical device that stores energy, just as a lead-acid battery. The major difference between the two is the plate material and electrolyte. Instead of using lead and lead dioxide plates with sulfuric acid, they use a metal oxide and carbon-based material for the plates and lithium salt for an electrolyte.

There are many advantages of lithium-ion over lead-acid batteries, including longer life expectancy and high power density, meaning they will take up less real estate. Lithium-ion can also operate at a higher temperature without degradation and are more efficient, taking less energy to recharge.

Lithium-ion batteries are susceptible to being over or under charge and must incorporate a battery monitoring system. This will reduce the need for maintenance but increases the upfront cost.

The major disadvantage of lithium-ion technology is the initial cost. In 2019, lithium-ion cost between 1.5 and three times that of VRLA batteries providing the same backup time. However, only a few years before that, they cost ten times more than VRLAs. As the technology matures and is used more widely, the cost will continue to decrease.

If the longer life and operation costs are factored over the life of a lithium-ion plant, they provide an advantage over VRLAs. The most cost-effective approach is to include lithium-ion batteries when replacing the UPS at the end of its life.

Conclusion

As I stated in the opening of this book, I hope you now have a better understanding of UPS systems and can speak the same language as others in the industry. The next time you need to decide on a UPS system for your critical equipment, I would hope you are comfortable in choosing what you need, or confident when speaking with the salesperson. When your current UPS system is serviced, or breaks, I hope you are now armed with the knowledge to understand what the technician is explaining and can ask follow-up questions if needed.

If you were to reread any of the case studies presented here, my hope is there is a better understanding and a similar incident does not happen to you.

Thanks for reading.
Rob
rob@robdelauter.com

Acknowledgments

As with any successful endeavor, a writer needs support, and this book is no different. Many people made this possible, but special thanks are owed to the following:

My life partner, best friend, and amazing wife, Ashley. First and foremost, thank you for your tolerance. Few have the patience to listen to me ramble on about things of no interest to them. But you would feign enthusiasm and encourage me to continue. You have my eternal gratitude for giving me the time and space I needed to complete this project. There are no words to express my appreciation for your support in all my efforts and, specifically, throughout the process of writing and publishing this book.

A special thanks to Ruth McFadden. There has been a no bigger cheerleader to my writing than you. Thank you for the encouragement you have given me over the years. Without you, this would not have been possible.

My mentors:

Andrew Nauman, for teaching me to constantly look deeper and ask why, and for keeping me on my toes, always learning. You have been my sounding board too many times to count.

Tom Wegemer, the finest boss I have ever had. You gave me the chance to make mistakes and learn from them. You taught me to be the best technician, engineer, and leader I can. Thank you for doing the first read-through of my manuscript, editing a rough draft into something I felt comfortable sending on.

My technical readers, Pete Laue and Tom Siedecki. Both of you took time from your busy lives to spend a few hours reading and commenting on the manuscript. Your comments gave me the confidence to move forward with publication.

My writing and publishing team:

Brian Rouff, your knowledge and experience in the writing and publishing process kept me on track. You have been there from the beginning with encouragement and guidance on the next steps when I got stuck.

Andy Meaden with Meaden Creative, for your work on the cover design, thank you. An even bigger thanks for the illustrations inside. I had no idea how I was going to complete them. Not only did you draw many of them, but you also provided me with direction on low-cost alternatives.

About the Author

Rob DeLauter began working in the critical power industry, specifically Uninterruptible Power Supply (UPS) systems, in 2000. He started his career as a service technician working for various manufacturers, performing startups, as well as preventive and corrective maintenance.

After completing his Bachelor of Science degree in Electrical Engineering from Capitol College in 2009, he performed site acceptances testing of UPS systems, batteries, and generators. He also enjoys troubleshooting complex power quality problems.

In 2012 Rob passed the Professional Engineering exam and is a registered Engineer in Maryland and Washington, D.C.

Rob works as the Operations Manager and a managing partner at Static Power Conversion Services, Inc. in Columbia, MD. The company specializes in providing custom solutions for customers ranging in size from IT closets to medium-sized data centers.

He enjoys writing and sharing the knowledge he has gained over his career to help educate others and solve similar problems. In addition to this book, he has written articles for *EC & M* magazine.

www.ingramcontent.com/pod-product-compliance
Lightning Source LLC
Chambersburg PA
CBHW040423100526
44589CB00022B/2817